THE END OF CHIRAQ

THE END OF CHIRAQ

Edited by Javon Johnson and Kevin Coval
with writers from Young Chicago Authors & Louder
Than a Bomb: The Chicago Youth Poetry Festival

NORTHWESTERN UNIVERSITY PRESS
EVANSTON, ILLINOIS

Northwestern University Press
www.nupress.northwestern.edu

Printed in the United States of America

10 9 8 7 6 5 4 3 2 1

Library of Congress Cataloging-in-Publication Data

Names: Johnson, Javon, editor. | Coval, Kevin, editor. | Young Chicago Authors
    (Organization), sponsoring body. | Louder Than a Bomb (Poetry slam),
    sponsoring body.
Title: The end of Chiraq : a literary mixtape / edited by Javon Johnson and Kevin
    Coval ; with writers from Young Chicago Authors & Louder Than a Bomb: The
    Chicago Youth Poetry Festival.
Description: Evanston, Illinois : Northwestern University Press, 2018. |
    Includes bibliographical references.
Identifiers: LCCN 2017059456 | ISBN 9780810137189 (pbk. : alk. paper) | ISBN
    9780810137196 (ebook)
Subjects: LCSH: African American youth—Illinois—Chicago—Social
    conditions—Literary collections. | African American youth—Illinois—
    Chicago—Social conditions. | Chicago (Ill.)—Social conditions—Literary col-
    lections. | Chicago (Ill.)—Social conditions. | High school students' writings,
    American—Illinois—Chicago.
Classification: LCC PS508.N3 E53 2018 | DDC 810.8/09283/0977311—dc23
LC record available at https://lccn.loc.gov/2017059456

Contents

A Tale of Two & Many Cities

Contesting the Narrative

The Culture Is the Art

The Future of Chicago

Javon Johnson

Preface

Chance the Rapper, whom *Rolling Stone* called "the most successful independent artist in popular music,"[1] shook up the music industry with his mixtapes. As the first artist to be nominated for and win a Grammy award for a streaming-only album—*Coloring Book*—his single "No Problem" is a testament to his refusal to sign with music labels, a highly political decision to play by a different set of rules. Hailing from the Chatham neighborhood in South Side Chicago, Chance has the world rethinking many traditional music industry models, as his music is a commitment to access, freedom, and an illustration that musical success is doable on self-made terms.

On the second track of his critically acclaimed *Acid Rap*, he says:

> It just got warm out, this this shit I've been warned about.
> I hope that it storm in the morning, I hope that it's pouring out.
> I hate crowded beaches, I hate the sound of fireworks.
> And I ponder what's worse between knowing it's over and dying first.

He drastically departs from the summer narratives of endless youth and joyous wonderment to illustrate the violence that has become synonymous with summertime Chicago and lament the seemingly inevitable loss of life. Switching from rap, he sings on:

> Cause everybody dies in the summer.
> Wanna say ya goodbyes, tell them while it's spring.
> I heard everybody's dying in the summer,
> so pray to God for a little more spring.

Chance's desire for a longer spring is an imaginative call for a world where the summers come later and are shortened. It is a creative attempt toward a different kind of intervention that looks beyond the state for help. Moving to a more practical plea, he ends the song by highlighting the neglect of certain parts of Chicago:

> I know you scared,
> you should ask us if we scared, too.
> If you was there,
> then we'd just knew you cared, too.

In this way, Chance the Rapper's mixtapes are not simply independent projects that challenge traditional music industry practices, they are celebration and critiques of his home city. His mixtapes, at times autobiographical and journalistic, are a creative attempt to augment what we know of Chicago's hood through a different type of showing. *The End of Chiraq: A Literary Mixtape* follows that very logic.

The End of Chiraq — "Chiraq" being an amalgamation of Chicago and Iraq — starts and ends with the idea that creativity is critical in imagining better possibilities. Rather than academic essays from theorists on high, we wanted to explore Chicago from what the critically acclaimed hip-hop group A Tribe Called Quest might call "low end theory." Taken from the title of Tribe's sophomore album, "low end theory" is perhaps an "Excursion," to cite the record's first track, where "you must be honest and true to the next" (Q-Tip, *The Low End Theory*, 1991). "Low end theory" is a doing in that it "make moves" and "never, ever, ever . . . fake moves" (Q-Tip). It is a praxis grounded in honesty and realness that recognizes when Q-Tip says he is "prominent like Shakespeare" he is invoking W. E. B. Dubois. In other words, Q-Tip suggests that he too sits "with Shakespeare and he winces not" (Dubois, *The Souls of Black Folk*). Taking both Q-Tip and Dubois's lead, we contend that the youth in this book are creatively theorizing in ways that "move arm in arm with Balzac and Dumas" (Dubois, *The Souls of Black Folk*). In this way, *The End of Chiraq* is collection of poems, lyrics, interviews, essays, and artwork, primarily from Chicago's youth, that expresses their concerns, views, and desires for Chicago's past, present, and future.

This edited collection came about as a result of a series of conversations. After accepting Harvey Young and Gianna Mosser's gracious offer to submit to *Second to None: Chicago Stories*, we wanted to produce a creative book about Chicago and problematize the term "Chiraq." We immediately agreed that the project should be youth driven, polyphonic, and multifaceted. By enlisting the work of Young Chicago Authors and their investigative wing, the Chicago Beat, we ensured that the book was not just about the Windy City, but would be a project that is from and of Chicago. These were, and are, a series of decidedly political moves explicitly arguing that youth voices matter, hood voices matter, and creativity — the thing that allows us to imagine beyond existing structures and modes — matters. In so saying, the best way to read this book is as a carefully curated literary mixtape of critically creative theories from and about Chicago.

In true mixtape fashion, we hope you engage this project with the same independent and boundary-challenging energy indicative of much of the art form. We hope you consume this in whole and in parts, and that you put your friends on to do the same. Make a "playlist" of your favorite works, re-read them, repeatedly, run them back, share them. Ask, "How do these young artists, scholars, and activists compel me to understand the complexities of Chicago, its pain, its possibilities, and its people, in different ways?"

This project was not simply the effort of two men; rather it came about through a network of brilliant people. We thank Young Chicago Authors, the Chicago Beat, the poets and teachers of Louder Than a Bomb: The Chicago Youth Poetry Festival and After School Matters, for their amazing contributions and their dogmatic belief that they deserve and can create a more just and equitable world. We especially want to thank the folks who did a lot of the heavy editorial lifting, Joshua Addams and Veronica Popp. In many ways, their names deserve to appear alongside our own. Thank you to each contributor, especially Haki Madhubuti and the publishers who granted us the rights to reprint some crucially important pieces here. Thank you to the assistants, Mickayla Johnson and Margaret Caldwell, for their diligence and hard work. Thank you to Gianna Mosser and Harvey Young, whose patience and guidance made all the difference.

Finally, thank you to Chicago, who, despite its problems, perseveres and soars.

Note

1. Sarah Grant, "What Chance the Rapper's Streaming-Only Grammy Nod Means for Pop's Future," *Rolling Stone*, February 10, 2017, https://www.rollingstone.com/music/features/what-chance-the-rappers-streaming-only-grammy-nod-means-w466125.

Javon Johnson

Intro

The End of Chiraq: A Literary Mixtape is a collection of poems, lyrics, essays, interviews, and artwork from Chicago's own that hopes to add to Chicago's rich history of creative world making. Thinking of this project as a literary mixtape is critical, as *The End of Chiraq* works to bring together an array of Chicago voices, especially those that, like the mixtape artist, "[take] place off the radar."[1] In the third chapter of his book *Why White Kids Love Hip Hop: Wankstas, Wiggers, Wannabes, and the New Reality of Race in America,* Bakari Kitwana dispels the myth that white males are 70 percent of hip-hop's audience by, among other things, looking at how black and brown youth made use of the mixtape. Gaining popularity throughout the 1980s, mixtapes are compilations of music for public and/or private consumption "in which a deejay creatively mixes emerging and established rap artists rhyming over unreleased and/or previously published music.[2] Without getting into the debates on piracy and intellectual property, mixtapes democratized music in how they have been historically unconcerned with mainstream outlets having control over production and distribution. In similar fashion, by bringing to light the voices of poets, rappers, activists, and visual artists who might otherwise be overlooked, *The End of Chiraq* seeks to democratize the discussion around Chiraq, as well as the bodies who live in the vibrant and sometimes violent neighborhoods of Chicago.

As kids of the 1980s, both Kevin Coval and I grew up making and sharing mixtapes. Save for the occasional mix created for a particular love interest, we both agree that the best mixes were those that had their fingers on the pulse of a specific space or time. Whether it was using DJ Jazzy Jeff & the Fresh Prince's "Summertime" to illustrate the unrepentant joys of summer, trading the Molemen's mixes along the "El" in Chicago, or Grandmaster Flash & the Furious Five's "The Message," Public Enemy's "Fight the Power," and N.W.A.'s "Fuck tha Police" to capture the angst of those in the Los Angeles Uprisings (also known as riots) of 1992, strong mixtapes are soundtracks that offer us aural cues, outlets, and coping mechanisms for critical moments and spaces in our lives. Following that logic, *The End of Chiraq* ambitiously attempts much of the same work in this edited volume about Chicago, Chiraq, and where the two are analogous and alien.

In the second verse of the hard-hitting "Murder to Excellence," Chicago native Kanye West lyrically claimed, "I feel the pain in my city wherever I go, 314 soldiers died in Iraq, 509 died in Chicago." In so doing, he effectively gut-punched us with statistics that jarringly compared one of the United States' major global cities to a country in the Middle East engulfed in war. As the tenth track on Jay-Z's and Kanye West's critically acclaimed *Watch the Throne* album, "Murder to Excellence" ambitiously discussed an array of topics from police murder, black-on-black crime, and nihilism to black love and mobility. Easily one of the most memorable lines from the song, and perhaps the album more generally, Kanye's comparison of Chicago and Iraq, though in now way novel, points to the violence plaguing what many call Chiraq.

"Chiraq" (Chicago + Iraq) is a term generated by Chicago's creative youth to mark the gun violence that is so rampant in in the City. Mostly due to underfunded schools, unequal access to labor markets, problematic policies, an unjust judicial system, redlining, and a near-tyrannical police force, Chicago's violence is so profound and prolific that it led to the creation of the infamous nickname Chiraq. Like the problematic myth of so-called black-on-black crime—which is to suggest not that black intraracial violence is unreal but that structural racism positions it as magically more aberrant than all other intraracial violence—critics have rightfully pointed out that the term "Chiraq" is employed to frame black and brown bodies as inherently pathological, destructive, and always in need of state intervention.

Dubbing the troubling moniker "urban lexicon," Chicagoan Natalie Y. Moore plainly states, "It's hard to pinpoint the origins of the term 'Chiraq.'"[3] Equally, it is incredibly difficult to precisely define the word. Some people wear the term, and the violence it symbolizes, as a badge of honor, another tough obstacle Chicagoans must endure. Some see it as a shameful reminder of Chicago's failures. Others see it as mix of both, waffle back and forth, or perceive it as something altogether different. Moore's issue with Chiraq is grounded in the moniker's nonchalant use, the sense of pride some take in it, and the ways in which those in power use it to construct Black and Brown as the enemy to be rooted out, because "in war," she asks, "what do you do with the enemy?"[4] In this way, equating a heavily black and brown American city with a real or imagined war zone opens up the space for harsh state-sanctioned intervention through police militarization, aggressive punitive measures, and the redistribution of much-needed resources, while simultaneously justifying the United States' continued colonial efforts in the Middle East.

More than two decades prior, part of Chicago's Albany Park neighborhood was dubbed "Little Beirut" as way to mark its violence and untenable living conditions. Located in the northwest of the city, 1980s Albany Park was one of the nation's most ethnically diverse neighborhoods and housed a significant number of people receiving governmental aid, and "its high concentration of large, multiunit apartment buildings owned by absentee landlords" made it "the gateway for new immigrants."[5] Following the Siege of Beirut in the summer of 1982, which was a part of a larger series of complex conflicts, occupations, battles, attacks, and discussions known as the Lebanese Civil War (1975–90), the fifteen-year combat and how the Middle East is troublingly constructed in the U.S. imaginary as always over there and always backward made Beirut seem like a place forever stuck in battle. In this way, nicknames such as Little Beirut and Chiraq serve to construct poor neighborhoods of color as always backward, not truly American, and deserving of militaristic takeovers much like U.S. occupation efforts throughout the Middle East.

However, Dwight Conquergood's potent and nuanced essay on Little Beirut, "Life in Big Red: Struggles and Accommodations in a Chicago Polyethnic Tenement," illustrates how neither violence, inhumane living conditions, exploitative landlords, nor state neglect can tell the complex stories of those who live in the so-called slums. Whether it was the courtyard kids of Big Red finding joyful ways to transform the otherwise unfriendly space, "doubling up" families in single units to cut the cost of rent, or other modes of kinship and caring, Conquergood informs us that people, especially those who have been and are disenfranchised by those in power, will always find ways to create for themselves a more livable world.

This framing of Chicago as a war zone proved so pervasive that filmmaker Spike Lee borrowed Chi-Raq as the title for his fictional film meditation on violence in the Windy City. Starring Nick Cannon, Wesley Snipes, Angela Bassett, Samuel L. Jackson, Teyonah Parris, Jennifer Hudson, and John Cusack, Lee, who wrote, produced, and directed the film, employed satire to comment on the bloodshed in the Windy City. Lee based the script on Lysistrata; as in Aristophanes's comedy, the women of Chicago withhold sex from their male lovers as a way to end gang violence. While Chi-Raq received positive reviews, many Chicagoans, including some of the writers that contributed this volume, felt the film was at best poorly executed and at worst a mockery of their lives.

Chance the Rapper, whom Christopher Weingarten of Rolling Stone said created "the richest hip hop album of 2016,"[6] took issue with Lee's Chi-Raq, even taking a shot by ending his verse on Kanye West's "Ultralight Beam" by quipping, "cause they'll flip the script on your ass like Wesley and Spike." The Chicago rapper, who also goes by "Little Chano from 79th," grew up in the Chatham neighborhood, currently has the hip-hop world at his feet with the release of his critically acclaimed independent mixtape-LP, Coloring Book, and he did not mince words when he called Spike Lee's movie sexist and racist in series of tweets. A highly passionate and decidedly political artist, Chance the Rapper speaks openly about the violence in Chicago, including the state-sanctioned murder of Laquan McDonald at the hands of Chicago police officer Jason Van Dyke when Little Chano called Van Dyke by name on *Saturday Night Live* during a transformative performance.

The consistent bloodshed, the recent release of Spike Lee's *Chi-Raq*, the ever-popular Kanye West, the meteoric rise of Chance the Rapper, as well as the lesser known but still incredibly political and unapologetic Vic Mensa and Mick Jenkins—all of whom (save for West) participated in Young Chicago Authors in their youth—make a book about Chicago and its violence both timely and urgent. Young Chicago Authors, or YCA, is a brilliant youth organization that "transforms the lives of young people by cultivating their voices through writing, publication, and performance education" and produced a dizzying cadre of teachers, intellectuals, activists, and artists of all varieties.[7] And that each of the aforementioned young rappers gained fame and notoriety partly due to their desire to lyrically discuss their politics and their visions for a better Chicago is a testament to the fact that young black and brown Chicagoans are far from nihilistic and that the city, and the nation more generally, is clamoring for more creative discussions about the Windy City and its violent crime.

Answering this call, we felt it important to ensure that a book about Chicago and Chiraq solely feature the work of Chicagoans. More, we wanted the City's youth, particularly the emerging artists and activists from YCA, to be the spine of this book, so that their energy and spirit lead the charge for a more livable and lovable world. YCA was founded in 1991 by Dr. Robert Boone as a way to address the dearth of resources for teenagers serious about writing. YCA, which now serves more than ten thousand Chicago teens every year, has grown well beyond Boone's workshops to offer free programming in poetry, hip-hop, journalism, and pedagogy, as well as a weekly open mic night. With a lofty mission to transform "the lives of young people by cultivating their voices through writing, publication, and performance education," YCA is a testament to the power of youth voices and how they are constantly speaking beyond what is to what could be. In this way, we want to show how young folks on the ground think and work toward new worlds, and in true mixtape fashion, we wanted to ensure that we included the so-called underground voices—that is, work produced by Chicago artists and activists who are not usually called to speak about their dreams and desires for their own home.

The young folks in this collection, who in true Chicago spirit are not waiting for failed and inept politicians but are themselves Chicago-ing—that is,

mobilizing, creating, and working toward a safer and more equitable city—
are using art and activism in an attempt to put an end to Chiraq. Taking our
cue from them, this book follows a rather straightforward path. Keeping in
mind Michel de Certeau's pithy phrase, "What the map cuts up, the story
cuts across,"[8] we tried to ensure that the poems and stories in this book cut
up Chicago and Chiraq in ways that challenge dominant narratives about
the City's poor and of-color youth, while providing the reader with a new per-
spective. However, rather than simply remapping the city, which is typically a
restructuring that leaves the dominant in power, we hope that the poems and
stories in *The End of Chiraq* move toward an abstraction of the city that works
to disrupt those power structures altogether. We want the reader to witness
the dreams and desires of young Chicagoans, to see them working toward
safer and more livable neighborhoods, in work that is not only about stopping
gun violence but also about taking to task problematic power structures that
defund schools, systematically disenfranchise, and deny equal access to labor
markets, all the while encouraging and supporting the mass imprisonment
of black and brown people. In this way, *The End of Chiraq* is broken up into
five parts.

The first section, "Welcome to Chiraq," features work that introduces what
Nile Lansana here calls "the Chiraq reality." Exploring Chiraq as a political
term and space, this section takes an innovative and intellectual look at the
violence in Chicago, as well as the violence in how Chicago is framed. "A
Tale of Two & Many Cities," the second section, addresses Chicago's "hy-
persegregation,"[9] how the state is a participatory agent in the city's violence,
and how even in the so-called violent parts, which as toaster quipped, "you
can ignore . . . If you're rich enough . . . [or] white enough," are too complex,
vibrant, and resilient to be reduced to a space of danger. The third section,
"Contesting the Narrative," takes aim at pop and popular depictions of the
Windy City, offering new ways to look at and think about how we discuss Chi-
cago. "The Culture Is the Art" and "The Future of Chicago," the fourth and
final sections of the book, compel us to think beyond Chiraq and take stock of
the creativity coming out of the so-called war zone and how people in Chica-
go are always already imagining, working toward, and creating a better future.
With pieces from Idris Goodwin, Haki Madhubuti, Nate Marshall, and Jami-
la Woods, we are invited, begged even, to consider how Chicago, despite the
violence, the segregation, the systemic disenfranchisement of certain groups,
or any of its other issues, is always able to start "a new day / a new life. [A] fresh
start," as thirteen-year-old Gellila Asmamaw tells us at the close of this book.
In structuring the book this way, we invite you to think about the violence *in*
Chicago and not the violence *as* Chicago. More importantly, we hope you

see the larger structural and systemic connections to the city's bloodshed, as opposed to nihilistic black and brown youth. In this way, we hope to show how so many youths are actively working to put an end to Chiraq.

We understand that as a concept and a term, "Chiraq" is not without its problems. However, we wonder if there is a way to see this term, which no doubt came from Chicago's ever-creative youth, as a way to frame Chicago's violence as equally state sanctioned and created in service of U.S. white imperialist capitalist desires, much like Iraq's. In other words, rather than dismissing the term wholesale, exploring it in multiple competing and contradicting facets might allow us to find something critically salvable and politically useful. While we do not have the answer to this query, *The End of Chiraq* explores Chiraq betwixt and between what sociologist Janet Abu-Lughod calls Chicago's "back stage city" and its "front stage façade."[10] Theorizing from the ground up—from the combat zone, so to speak—this collection is not a definitive project, nor is it a genealogy or history of Chiraq; rather it is a critical and creative opportunity to unpack the vexed, and vexing, term.

There is a rather large mural of Jeff "J-Def" Abbey Maldonado Jr. in the Pilsen neighborhood of Chicago. Hand painted by mononymous Chicago artist Pablo, in conjunction with the Maldonado family, the Pilsen neighborhood, After School Matters, Pros Arts Studio, National Able Network, Inc., and the Resurrection Project, to "help keep his memory alive so that he's not just another statistic or another murder in Chicago," the mural forces the city to face, pun intended, the violence that plagues the city, which ultimately claimed J-Def's life.[11] In this way, the mural is about J-Def's murder and Chicago's violence more generally, using art as a means to work through and past the violence and, as Pablo quipped, "who controls the way our neighborhood looks and the messages that are conveyed." Pablo's larger-than-life painting is a visual rhetoric and requires a particular literacy, a knowledge of Chicago and its public art, to truly understand how it works to address simultaneously the violence and how the city is a player in its own destruction.

J-Def was a poet, rapper, and graffiti artist who "worked at the local After School Matters digital-photography job-training program for teens and was about to start his second year at Harold Washington College before transferring to Columbia College to study music."[12] By most accounts, he was a good person who was murdered the day after his nineteenth birthday due to mistaken identity. The mural of J-Def is one of many that memorialize the dead, beautify a city far too often rendered nihilistic, and use art as a world-making device to imagine a new, more livable city. J-Def, whose legacy and art endures, was one of those young critically creative Chicagoans we would have loved to include in this text. Now, just a few short blocks from the site of his murder, the erected mural stands, transforming the space of danger, pain, and hate to one of love.

The End of Chiraq aspires to a similar abiding aesthetic of transformative love. For me, love is a political act, an ever-renewing and renewable commitment to live a more ethical and connected life. It is the constant building of a more just world in which we could all collectively live our fullest and healthiest lives. Love is real work that does something; it is the materialization of our imagination of and desire for a better world. This collection is a love offering that gestures at, speaks to, and works toward a fully livable Chicago by demanding an end to Chiraq.

Notes

1. Bakari Kitwana, *Why White Kids Love Hip Hop: Wankstas, Wiggers, Wannabes, and the New Reality of Race in America* (New York: Civitas, 2006), 91.

2. Ibid.

3. Natalie Y. Moore, "The 'Chiraq' War Mentality in Chicago Prevents Solutions," *The Root*, January 6, 2014; http://www.theroot.com/the-chiraq -war-mentality-in-chicago-prevents-solution-1790874005.

4. Ibid.

5. Dwight Conquergood, "Life in Big Red: Struggles and Accommodations in a Chicago Polyethnic Tenement," in *Cultural Struggles: Performance, Ethnography, Praxis* (Ann Arbor: University of Michigan Press, 2013).

6. Christopher R. Weingarten, "Chance the Rapper's *Coloring Book* Is a Gospel-Rap Masterpiece," *Rolling Stone*, May 13, 2016; http://www .rollingstone.com/music/features/chance-the-rappers-coloring-book-is-a -gospel-rap-masterpiece-20160513.

7. See http://youngchicagoauthors.org/purpose/mission/.

8. Michel de Certeau, *The Practice of Everyday Life* (New York: Columbia University Press, 1984), 129.

9. The term "hypersegregation" was coined by Douglas S. Massey and Nancy A. Denton in their book *American Apartheid: Segregation and the Making of the Underclass* (Cambridge, Mass.: Harvard University Press, 1998).

10. Janet Abu-Lughod, *New York, Chicago, Los Angeles: America's Global Cities* (Minneapolis: University of Minnesota Press, 2000).

11. GCE Lab School, "J-Def Peace Project," September 20, 2011; https:// vimeo.com/29413343.12. Jane Leyderman, "Unhappy Birthday: The Murder of Young Artist J-Def Is Not the End of His Story," *New City*, September 22, 2009.

THE END OF CHIRAQ

Andrew Barber

on hearing King Louie

I don't remember when I first heard the term *Chiraq*, but I do remember what made me never forget it. April 21, 2011. King Louie, who was just starting to bubble up in the Chicago scene, dropped one of (in this writer's opinion) his best projects to date. It was titled *Chiraq, Drillinois*. A clever play on words, which further spiked my interest in the Chicago rapper. At the time, I wrote in my post, "Greatest. Mixtape. Title. Ever."

In 2011, *Drill* wasn't yet a bad word. Neither was *Chiraq*. The world hadn't had time to digest either of them. *Drill* was a verb before it became a genre of music. Did it have negative connotations? Sometimes. But it wasn't always a negative term. That is, until the press got hold of it.

The term *Drill* was coined by King Louie's good friend and fellow rapper Pacman, who was affiliated with the L.E.P. Bogus Boys. Sadly, Pacman never got the chance to see his term go global or turn into a genre of music, as he was tragically murdered in June of 2010—two full years before the Drill craze swept the music business.

By 2012, Drill had taken the world by storm. Fans, press, and publications became obsessed with artists such as Chief Keef, King Louie, and Lil Durk, who would go on to define the genre. This is when the term *Chiraq* took off as well.

The word *Chiraq* became polarizing. Some used it to describe the city they called home—wearing it as a badge of honor, while others called it a disgrace to their beautiful city. Sure, Chicago had its fair share of problems, but what big city doesn't?

Pro- and anti-*Chiraq* campaigns both took flight, and the city became divided—much like its hip-hop scene. *Chiraq* quickly became a cool buzzword for out-of-towners looking to cash in on the tumultuous scene. A half-dozen documentaries were made using the title, and Spike Lee even had the balls to come here and film a motion picture under the name (I still can't believe that didn't get shut down).

In 2016, the term *Chiraq* lives in purgatory. Many still use it. Most still hate it. But it's never going away. It's become synonymous with Chicago—and will be forever. Other cities have even jumped on the trend of naming their city after a war-torn Middle Eastern country (see Napganistan, a.k.a. Indianapolis). So yes, Chicago continues to push trends, even if it's a trend we don't necessarily like. Word to Keith Cozart.

Chiraq is dead. Long live Chiraq.

Kevin Coval

when King Louie first heard the word *chiraq*

2010

it was so hot
freezers became   furnaces.
               all the cheese
 melted from spicy chips.
 everybody's hands were red.
the air
 a sleeping bag
of blood.
 shoes dangled on telephone wires
like missiles
 toes
tigers. pick one
block everybody
know somebody
who not
a body
anymore.
        King Louie
must've been coming out the bag
of a crown royal, purple velour wrapped
round his hand, bands, knots, a split
swisher, sweet about his mane of wool.
eyes a flame, feet dipped in Bronze
nikes like the ville, the fire. this time

a kid might've said it slick.
a little cousin, cuzo
making a geo-political assessment,
a vernacular ingenuitious flip
& critical pronouncement
when addressing the amount
of violence & bodies
& occupying forces

responsible for the bodies
& violence & militarization
of the block. desert eagles
food deserts. countering
the myth of intervention:
the war on drugs, enduring
freedom, weapons of mass
desecration. some little son,
some little body dropped
                    this Chiraq
out the mouth
like a screwdriver,
running from forces far
greater & better
funded, more insidious
& sadistic.
 & King Louie
mighta waited on the block
to clear, for the heat to dissipate
like october, the lights to chill
like dusk, as this shiny gem
layed in the street like someone
 lost a dead
president but didn't know it.
he scooped it in his pocket.
touched its smooth Black earth
like obsidian, this history & death
he held close, anticipating the right
moment to share, to say it like a spell,
a whisper he plucked from air & was keeping
for the fall
to come

Mariame Kaba

To Live and Die in "Chiraq"

"Michael's been shot," the voice on the phone says.
"He's alive. He'll recover."
I breathe . . . easier;
temporarily relieved.

Michael is eighteen and on borrowed time. He reminds me regularly that he's not long for this world. I've heard the words (in some variation) so often that they now pour off me like water from a showerhead. What is the antidote to this certainty about one's impending death? I've lost my tongue. I want to break my silence to say that I love him and would be devastated if he didn't live until he is (at least) one hundred. But I don't respond. I pretend that I don't hear the words. I am numb and I can't guarantee that he will live to become an old man. He's young, black, poor, and living on the West Side of Chicago. I steel myself for bad news every morning, and this time it arrives.

Michael belongs to the tribe of the young and the unmoored. His body is passing through and he has no expectations of staying. We rode on the L together once. Michael's voice boomed throughout the trip. I asked him to lower it. He looked at me for a moment and kept loud-talking. I was embarrassed at his display and felt disrespected that he ignored my request. As soon as we got off the L, his voice returned to its normal decibel level. I asked why he spoke so loudly on the train. His response: *"I want them uncomfortable and they need to know that I was here."* My anger dissipated, and I've never forgotten his words. They are seared in my mind: *"They need to know that I was here."* We've never spoken of what it's like to feel "not here."

It's part of a now-familiar ritual for those who live or have lived in Chicago. The press reports on shootings and homicides with almost no context (historical or otherwise). Faceless and sometimes nameless numbers are tallied like baseball box scores. And this is fitting in its own way. The prurient voyeuristic sensational coverage is its own sport. Seven shots fired. The boy was hit five times. Fifteen other people riddled with bullets today. Four dead. It's not yet midnight.

After a couple of decades when overall shootings and homicides in Chicago were consistently decreasing, the last couple of years have seen a rise

9

in shootings from a historically low base. If you ask people living in the most marginalized communities in Chicago, they will tell you that violence is at record levels and untenable. Their perceptions are (comparatively but not in the aggregate) accurate because there is a growing crime and violence (separate but overlapping issues) gap in Chicago. Researcher Daniel Hertz (2013) suggests a plausible explanation for the gap between actual numbers and perception: "Over the last twenty years, at the same time as overall crime has declined, the inequality of violence in Chicago has skyrocketed."[1] Hertz was interviewed about the concept of inequality of violence, and he expounded on the idea:

> It's always been unequal. Everybody who lives in Chicago or knows anything about Chicago knows that there's a big gap in many indicators of quality of life, broadly speaking between richer neighborhoods on the North Side and poorer neighborhoods on the South and West Side, and has been for a very long time. But that gap in terms of violent crime has gotten much, much worse. In the early '90s, the most dangerous part of the city had about six times as many homicides as the safest third of the city. Today that number is about 15 times.[2]

Chicago is still one of the most segregated cities in the country, and patterns of violence reflect that segregation. How safe you feel in Chicago very much depends on your race and class positions.[3] The violence experienced by young people of color in the city is multidimensional—both interpersonal and structural. So many of the young have to swallow their rage as they are surveilled in stores and on the streets, as they are targeted by cops for endless stops and frisks, as they are denied jobs, as their schools are closed, and as they are locked in cages by the thousands. For some, the violations and the deprivation turn outward. The instrumental use of violence by some young people becomes a rational adaptive strategy in response to racial and economic oppression. For some of the young people I've worked with, the specter of death is a constant companion. A young man who has been behind bars for most of his formative years has told me on more than one occasion that he was always certain his life only held two viable possibilities: "die in the streets or die in prison."

The failures of every Chicago institution (schools, government, law enforcement, and more) pile up and crush hope. The cops spin tall tales to distract and to justify more violence. New Chicago police superintendent Eddie Johnson recently told an assembled crowd: "When I started as a patrolman in 1988, the average age of our shooters [was] nineteen, twenty years old. . . . Right now, the average is fifteen, sixteen years old." His words are deceptive; the average age of young people who sometimes commit violence with guns is between twenty-one and twenty-two. Eddie conjures baby "super-predators." What purpose does the lie serve? Is it to make children into enemy combatants whose deaths shouldn't be mourned? Isn't the truth dramatic enough?

In this city they've renamed "Chiraq," young black men live precariously. The act of renaming the stolen land upon which they live, considered to be agency by some, perversely seals their fate. "Chiraq" is a war zone that invites outsiders to offer their prescriptions for how to "solve" the problem of violence. In "Chiraq," community voices are drowned out. Community members become enemies or victims without agency or expertise on their own lives. "Chiraq" conditions how we think of ourselves and our neighbors. It traps us into considering solutions that are steeped in a punishment mindset. Adopting war zone metaphors puts a ceiling on our imaginations and constrains how we might address violence and harm. After all, you respond to tanks with more artillery and not with a peace circle. Restorative or transformative justice requires us to build trust and to establish relationships. This is difficult to do in "war zones," where suspicion and lack of trust are the order of the day.

"Chiraq" obliterates solidarity and invites (more) assaults. Politicians and other civic "leaders" unironically call for the National Guard to be deployed and martial law imposed to quell violence they've co-created. What the proponents of this so-called antiviolence strategy fail to appreciate is that the Chicago Police Department (CPD) is already one of the most militarized forces in the world. More police and martial law will not end violence. If anything, they exacerbate violence for far too many young people.

It's understandable why so many people rely on war metaphors. They hope that it will convey urgency and seriousness of purpose. It's an attempt to make violence against black people legible. But black people (in particular) are not seen as human—therefore the urgency sought is by definition unattainable. The government and its representatives will not be rushing any time soon to provide needed resources (living-wage jobs, good schools, free healthcare, recreational opportunities, and more). Without a mass movement, they won't implement the policies and programs that give young black people in Chicago the belief that they matter and will have a future. Black lives have been and are unfortunately seen as disposable. And by using war language, black people are further oppressed (if that's possible). They are only flesh to be acted upon, casualties of a profoundly antiblack world.

I visit Michael in the hospital. I hate hospitals. He smiles wanly. I burst into tears. The temporary relief I feel is quickly replaced by dread that can't be dislodged from the pit of my stomach. I worry about retaliation. I worry about Michael. This is a young man living in exile in his own country. His humanity is unacknowledged. He languishes in a place that Richard Wright has called "No Man's Land." He is allowed no feelings. He is just a threat: all of our fears rest on and in him. I remember our ride on the L and his words to me: *They need to know that I was here.* I realize that he is demanding to be "seen" by the larger world. Maybe the gun is his way of writing himself into our national story with a pen dipped in blood: an urgent message from a metaphorical war zone called Chiraq.

Notes

1. Daniel Hertz, "We've Talked about Homicide in Chicago at Least One Million Times but I Don't Think This Has Come Up" (blog post), August 5, 2013, http://danielkayhertz.com/2013/08/05/weve-talked-about-homicide-in-chicago-at-least-one-million-times-but-i-dont-think-this-has-come-up.

2. Quoted in Noah Berlatsky, "How Chicago Points to a Growing Inequality of Urban Violence," *CityLab*, October 3, 2013, http://www.citylab.com/equity/2013/10/how-chicago-points-growing-inequality-urban-violence/7103/.

3. Noah Berlatsky, "How Bad Is Violence in Chicago? Depends on Your Race," *Atlantic*, September 26, 2013, http://www.theatlantic.com/national/archive/2013/09/how-bad-is-violence-in-chicago-depends-on-your-race/280019/; Steve Bogira, "Concentrated Poverty and Homicide in Chicago," *Chicago Reader*, July 26, 2012, http://www.chicagoreader.com/Bleader/archives/2012/07/26/concentrated-poverty-and-homicide-in-chicago.

Malcolm London

Rome Wasn't Built in a Day

Chicago has emerged
a duplication of Rome,
a colosseum
for worldwide spectators,
eyelashes stapled to eyebrows
corneas wide & waiting
on the next tribune article
on the latest
body count
millions
of viewers
anxious to hear the next
bang bang from the pistol
mouths of Black boys

the applause for more audio
an audience of jackals
cackling & cheering on the symphony
of corpse pile up
in chicago
every tongue is mimicking
the art of the barrel, barrels of blood
& burials of young
through youtube videos
hip hop blogs, radio play
glory chasing boys
singing songs of drug trade,
& gun range, of home.

they are gladiators
fighting on a battlefield
where the landmines
police   news anchors   schools
yet when the gladiator tells his own story
                                        he blows up.

chief keef got signed to interscope
with a movie deal,
chiraq trended on twitter
as a joke
13 year rapper lil mouse
is on wayne's mixtape. this the dedication
we have for this music blasting
Black death, bullets & Chicago
we love to dance to it
we love to listen to it
it's so real, so hood
so real, *surreal.*

black death bullets & chicago
it is happening, it is urgent
more bodies being added to the list of *#3hunna*
there is no ignoring this.
and we don't. we turn up
this music louder than a mother's cry
for her funeral home children
we glorify.

but who benefit from this
no mother, no brother, no sister,
no son, no daughter, no aunt,
no uncle, no grandma, no granddad,
no father, no cousin, no homie
no rapper likes to write
eulogies.
who benefits from this
arena of black boys
with spears for hearts
armor skin
& crowds chanting for tombstones

south & west side
don't enjoy building new graveyards

while we dance on top
who benefit from this
who on top
who took our love and hip hop
and turned it into love and hip hop atlanta
we ratchet, we hood, we laugh
like we not wrapped in body bags
rap about body bags, gold
chains, and decked out chariots
who benefit from this
these gladiators don't
sleep on skeletons
just because they have a bone to pick.

our hoods cesspools
of blood and violence
but who
city planners,
who profit
from this colosseum
of black boy gladiators celebrated for their carnage
murdering for the world to watch.

Aneko Jackson

Memories

Remember how Summer Time Chicago used to be?
As I walk down the street,
My childhood replays itself
In front of me.
Juke Parties.
The Bud Billiken.
And chips was fo' fo' a dolla.
Broken fire hydrants for those who didn't want to go to the pool
And courts was full of boys shootin hoops.
Parents teaching me to step at the family bbq.
And as I got older,
My childhood must have took a wrong turn at a corner
Cause it ain't like that no more
Chicago became Chiraq
And little boys be afraid to be Black.
The only gang they fear is the one who wears the badge.
Summer Time Chi ain't nothing but a distant memory of nostalgia & bliss
And things you miss.
Sometimes I want to live in my memories.
A sudden tap on my back snatches me out of my reverie
And instantly I'm back
To a War in Chiraq

Nile Lansana

Windowpain
Bryce Thomas

79th & Cottage Grove:
My YouTube channel
Devil be only subscriber
Wi-Fi eludes me
Find my connections in concrete
These streets give different signals

Password required to enter this colorful chaos. Outside
Brothers exchange codes quick and complex
Hands flow frantic

No mistakes

you gon look fake

Mean mug

you gon look soft

Pursed lips

you's a snitch

Bring the clip

you's a . . .

All these
Young dark skinned dreams surround me
Deferred by deliberate destruction

Teacher tries to silence me   I speak louder
Eyes dilated by visions of the Eiffel
But if I can't break this windowpain
Closest this nigga gon get to Paris is
Watch the Throne

I watch my streets on fire like MJ in the fourth
Those ain't the only shots 'round these courts
Can't find the satire

In my homie's coffin
Maybe it's deep
In his mama's shrieks
Next week
Shoulda turned 18
Last words on replay
"Homie you tweakin'"

At least there's another bed for his six little brothers and sisters to sleep in

Every soldier in 773 prays

Let me see my grandchillun
Before I'm slain

Everyday we struggle
To break this windowpain

Demetrius Amparan

My grandmother tells me and my cousins why she hates the word *Chiraq* . . .

Mixing culture for the sake of chaos is a sin
punishable under the dominion of our lord.

No sunday school can teach the proper technique
for washing blood off your skin.

you niggas
need more respect for your niggas

And more respect for your god.

He worked too hard on your flesh for it to burn
from anything but his sun.

My grandmother is a remnant of our great migration north.
She double-dutches city blocks like the color lines are still there

A creature of habit.

She doesn't know that helps her
dodge the bullets.

She doesn't understand our infatuation with
Black death

As old as a john wayne film
On her turn style television.

She still fries her chicken on cast iron skillets
Loves when the lard pops onto her wrists

Like shackles breaking
Like freedom is only a compass north.

My grandmother likes to pretend she doesn't hear us swear
She likes it better when we are angels,
Like most seem to.

my grandmother thinks the word chiraq
is a rude way of insulting her

because she cried on 9/12
the day her favorite food and liquor nearly burned to ash.

Chiraq sounds like you niggas
need directions
north.

these "terrorists"
got the only lottery
and meat for five miles
& you niggas wanna play with fire and god.

Mixing culture for the sake of chaos is a sin.
Mixing culture for the sake of love . . .

now that god's work.

Page May

Do we even need to be understood to get free?

I am an outsider, born and raised in rural Vermont. As such, I can only ask questions about its meanings and its implications. I am not here to draw conclusions.

I first came to hear the term "Chiraq" through the mainstream news. Pundits lamented, horrified but mesmerized. They described a growing epidemic of violence; gangs, guns, and death. It was Black. It was brutal. It was out of control. Apparently, it could only be described as a war zone. This mainstream narrative does remind me of Iraq, but not in the intended ways.

Since moving here, I have learned that, before it was mainstream, "Chiraq" came out of young Black people describing their experiences as young Black people in Chicago. It is a complicated term for a complicated situation. At least one nuance of "Chiraq" names the relationship between young Black people and the State. The City and its army (the Chicago Police Department) disinvest, displace, criminalize, and terrorize Black Chicagoans. The State uses the law, the budget, and its monopoly on violence and "justified force" to degrade Black life. This is not a war among/between Black people, as the news outlets reported, but a war waged by the State against Black people. The difference is telling. And I think the Iraq War is a good example as to why.

Over time, the Iraq War came to be understood and described in mainstream circles less and less as a war between the US government and the Iraqi people, and more a U.S. intervention into a long, increasingly dangerous civil war between religious groups. The role of the U.S. government, the U.S. military, and U.S. imperialism in creating and maintaining those conditions was not questioned. When a majority of people understand a conflict as random chaos between communities, the State has a much easier time justifying a militarized invasion. And they hide the blood on their hands under clever misnomers like the "War on Terror" or the "War on Drugs." This leads to the question, What does the State achieve from a mainstream perception of Chicago as "Chiraq"?

Another noteworthy similarity I see between narratives around Chicago/ Chiraq and Iraq / War on Terror is a lack of context: The violence taking place is senseless, ahistorical, inevitable, and unending, no beginning and no end. There is no humanity or agency to the situation. No analysis of power.

No roots. There is no sense that choices were made that led to this moment. But of course, every condition, every conflict has roots and a history. And to ignore those is very dangerous. The mainstream use of the term "Chiraq" to describe Chicago strategically taps into the depoliticized narration of the Iraq War. It produces a negative feedback loop—for both Chicago *and* Iraq—that erases the politics, agency, humanity, and resistance involved. Isn't that suspiciously convenient for a State trying to cover the blood on its hands?

My last question is one that comes up regularly for me, as an organizer in the Black Lives Matter movement.

Oppression is worldwide, though it is not simple or homogenous. The problems that we experience as Black people are not superior, but they are specific. They are tangible, they are palpable, they are real, they are material. They have names. Why then, do we feel the need to articulate our struggle through metaphor? We seek empathy from a world that has never recognized our humanity, and so, to bridge the gap, we are compelled to attach ourselves to other peoples' struggles. It's a kind of appropriation rooted in a desperation to be legible. As if the only thing keeping us from freedom is the rest of the world's belief in our suffering. I identify with this compulsion and am guilty of it too. But I think if we want to get free more than we want to be understood or affirmed, we must question the limitations of this approach. What is lost in translation when we mimic another's grammar of suffering? When you are only understood through metaphor, are *you* really understood? Do we even need to be understood to get free?

Fatimah Asghar

9 of Disks

the Tarot Card representing enjoyment, gain,
& indulgence in your happiness & work

Gain the bearded man tells me
& my eyes turn green. It's November

& the color is everywhere around me.
I could forget I live in Chicago

where the winter plays a dead game
breaks my window with its knuckles.

It's November & nearly 80 degrees
The trees are showing off again

dressed up like *jalaybee* & caution tape.
I could forget I live in Chicago.

A few blocks south, a 9 year old boy
was executed in an alleyway early

this week. I see him in the headlines.
The articles say they found his basketball

the one he always carried with him
at the mouth of the street. Everywhere

children are dying. & everywhere
I see them living too. My students

whose laughter rips through the halls
who throw their arms around me

when they walk in the door. How
can it be November & sunny?

Where did the boy go? What cloud
is holding his body? How can we

get him back? *Enjoy,* the cards say.
But who am I to be happy?

Who am I to be brown & alive?
Can I trade my card?

Can we get him back?

Interview by Aneko Jackson

Frank Bradely

I asked if he wanted to come in, because it was cold. He declined, twice. After a third time, after I noticed he was shivering, he gave in and accepted a seat on the couch. When I apologized for the clutter, he told me that he lived in dirt, so there is nothing to be ashamed of. He took off his orange coat. I took a closer look. He was covered in tattoos, a five-point star on the middle of his neck. Life for him has been tumultuous. Outside, he had to deal with the streets. Inside, he dealt with domestic violence between his mother and father. Frank Bradely, twenty-one, has done a lot of living.

Frank spent most of his early childhood in the Robin Taylor Projects. "It was boring and nasty. I don't really remember. We had rats and roaches. Crack pipes and trash on the staircases. The only good thing was that family came together."

Throughout adolescent years, Frank did a lot of relocating around various areas of the city but managed to stay on the South Side. After leaving the Taylor homes, Frank moved around 93rd and Buffalo. "It was good. I went on field trips [at school]. In my eyes, it was good."

Frank opened up about having to witness domestic violence in his home. "I watched my dad hit my mom. It was a lot of yelling. It was regular life. I grew up wanting to protect my mom. Watching situations I don't like talking about. It was stressful."

Toward the end of his grammar school days, he moved to 93rd & Blackstone.

But by the age of fifteen, Frank had moved to his fifth house, located on 111th & Parnell. His father had left, and Frank was helping his mother. When he left, Frank says that the stress of life left with him. But at seventeen, he moved to 71st & Maplewood. "It was turnt. I was having fun, getting more experiences. Buying my own shit. Providing for myself."

At nineteen, he was back over east. Life changed again once his mother got a boyfriend. Frank isn't too fond of the new male figure in their life. "It was bogus. My OG put a nigga before me. I don't like it or her BF."

Now, Frank lives in Englewood. When I asked him if Englewood was as bad as they say, he replied, "I don't know. People die every day." He asked could he smoke a "square" during the interview. To that, I obliged. He pulls out a cigarette, lights it, and takes a long, heavy drag.

Continuing the interview but taking a turn in subject, I ask him if he is in a gang. He looks at me and laughs like I asked him a ridiculous question. "Yea, of course. GD. Growing up with my dad, I was around eight or nine. I don't focus on gangbangin' though."

Frank says he was blessed (initiated) in a clique. When I ask which one, his body goes rigid. "I don't want to tell you." He finishes his cigarette and shifts back toward me. I ask him when was it that he first heard the term "Chiraq." He says he was about eighteen, and he first heard through rap, from artists like Chief Keef and Lil Jojo.

Frank sees "Chiraq" as the area of Chicago ranging from 27th and State to the "wild hunnids." Frank openly expresses his love for the Chicago, but sees the notoriety it has gotten because of the term as problematic. "I love my city to be known, but now people look at us as killas."

For Frank, fighting and robbing people has been a part of his young life, but he isn't for the amount of killing that has been going on. He's been to jail before, for making "a wrong mistake, and hanging around the wrong people." For him, jail was not the place to be, and he knows he never wants to go back there. He says that because of his dreads, a common hairstyle for some of the drillas around the city, he has been mistaken for people doing "the bad stuff." He also mentions that he has experienced police brutality before. "As far as being stopped & frisked and being talked to badly, yea. All that other shit, nah."

Frank believes that a bit of divine intervention got him on the right path. "Prayer works, at the end 2012 into 2013. I broke my house arrest band, I had a dirty drop, on the run for four months, and I had caught another case. I went to school while I was in jail, when I went to see my judge at my court hearing they threw my case out. My prayer worked."

I ask him what he would rename "Chiraq" if he could. He says Chicago. I ask him why, and he says, "I don't know, I don't have another name for it." He becomes silent momentarily, and it is apparent that he is deep in thought. He goes to say, "The only reason why they call it Chi-Raq, bodies drop like I-Raq."

I ask Frank what he is focused on now. He replies, "Getting myself together. I am proud of myself because I am going to get my high-school diploma, I have a job, and [am] taking care of my daughter. Focusing on myself is what I'm trying to do."

Frank says that he has thought about leaving Chicago, moving "to Florida or Cali, winning the lottery and getting the fuck on."

Jacqui Germain

How America Loves Chicago's Ghosts More Than the People Still Living in the City
An Erasure Poem

using the lyrics of Chance the Rapper's "Paranoia"

Eyes been on the gun,

on the dying,

the shit neighborhood.

They watch the paper,

watch the hood boy militia

trapped in the middle of the sun.

Lips with a lotta murder talk.

They probably scared of all the

dark dark down here. Our nation,

dry eyes, paranoia and a lotta dying,

been pouring fireworks in the summer.

I hear everybody's god

a little scared too.

A TALE OF TWO
+ MANY CITIES

Patricia Frazier

I Am Windy City

after Jayne Cortez's "I Am New York City"

i am windy city. here is my tomato head.baton.scattered badge and blue.
i got my cousins ears.of corn gentrifrying in the melting pot. my mouth a
mercury lake i baptized jean baptiste in.a barn fire. I am windy city of red
meat. stocked yards.of men in factories.inside my belly a jungle of segregat-
ed joints. rub my navy pores with the blood of betadine boys. making steel
and stealing it. i am windy city of cabrini green.giants. hear my newport
throat croak an eight hour work day. a haymarket rally in the projects. pipe
bomb at pullman's pied piper. i work for no one.

i am windy city of blood-
y gums. my teeth a collection of patina coated churches. my ferris wheel
earrings too chicana for the rest of white ass illinois. my boys cleansed the
white city with a storm of gunpowder tears. i am windy city only dressed in
white on valentine's for all my lovers
massacred at the hands of chiraq. a man i don't know who keeps trying to
wife me.
chiraq is boo boo da fool and the foolish who bool with peeping toms who
have license to stripsearch. chiraq turn churches into resale gun stores.
chiraq a trap song serenade sung into the wrong ear. chiraq city of lost.boys
under the hood. chiraq could never.take my face value of royal flush.into
the chicago river. my leaning sears tower of pizza. my heineken and soul-
food.gout.feet tap dancing barefoot.with my hotheaded friends. my confetti
fleshed comrades. come break bread with me.

toaster

FAKE

when you meet someone outside of Chicago
and they tell you they're from Chicago
they're from joliet
evanston
probably shaumberg

which means they're lying to you
which means the person you've just met
is already lying to you

for evidence's sake ask the fake *what part*
they will say *part of what*

and you'll say *Chicago,*
*that's what this **whole** conversation was about*
why is this suddenly confusing?
and they'll say
uhhhhhhhhhhhh
as in
uhhhhhhh downtown
or
uuhhhhhhhh Wriggley Field
or
uuuuuuuuuuuuuuuuuuuuuuuuuuhhhhhhhhhh the lake?

if they respond with
just thirty minutes outside the city
that's not the city
because it takes thirty minutes to get there
from where ever the fuck they live
outside the city

if they say *east side*
they're from rockford illinois

gary indiana
china

fake-chicagoans are always asking for directions
fake-chicagoans are always walking on the wrong side of the
street
fake-chicagoans don't say excuse me when they bump into you
because fake-chicagoans don't know enough
to be polite
to real
live
actual Chicagoans
who are well within our rights to fuck "fake-chicagoans" up
which is how you can tell someone's from Chicago :
they'll fuck you up

on GP
which stands for "General Principle"
which means "for no good goddamn reason"
because people get fucked up in Chicago for no reason all the time
and it's never a tourist

and people move to Chicago anyway
like their life's in danger
like their life is worth more when it's in danger
as if their life was ever in danger
like trauma is a fashion statement they can take it off when it's too cold

and yes
the people who moved to Chicago
technically live in Chicago

but fuck them

they are not real Chicagoans
they started somewhere else
and no one gives a shit about that place
because when someone from
wherever they're from

comes to visit
they say things like

no no no i live in the good parts of Chicago
which means
the safe parts
which means
the north side
which means
away from brown people

which is a lie
because there are all sorts of brown people on the north side
and none of them are safe

however
fake-chicagoans aren't lying to themselves
because for them
chicago is a place where you can ignore what you'd rather not see
if you're rich enough
if you're white enough

so rich white people love chicago
rich white people are moving to chicago
and they tell all their new vacation friends the "truth"
which is

i'm from chicago
when they should say
i live near chicago
or
i am the bringer of starbucks
and walgreenz
and whole foods
and condos
and cops
or
i'll risk a black man's life for a noise complaint

or

Aneko Jackson

Concrete Flowers

Being from Chicago is like being a flower growing from concrete. And there's a tree soaking all the sun. Walking down the street, liquor stores and churches plant themselves on every block. You have to see the beauty in people who drink their sorrows away Saturday night, then wake up the following morning to praise the man who encouraged them to make it through the week. You have to see the beautiful in the ugly. The neighborhood drug dealers who loiter on store fronts, munch on chips and a honeybun. Unable to get a job because of petty crimes they committed before graduating grammar school: they stand there and eat. You have to see the beauty in their ability to process numbers with their lack of slumber.

Watching the mother who struggles day to day who can make $1 out of 15¢. Or make meals out of corn meal & canned goods. Watching her teach, nurse, babysit, and advise her children After she lays them down to sleep, she cries. She is late on rent. Again. You have to see the beauty behind a tear, a prayer. The picture of her grandmother hanging on the wall above her head seems to work miracles throughout the night.

The student, who learns despite there being no books. Ridiculed because the shoes aren't the newest. Eating the disgusting school lunch, the student is grateful. Managing homework on an empty stomach, but when the student receives their report card, their pride is full. You cannot tell me there ain't beauty in the hood. The hood is resourceful even with a lack of resources. The flower sprouting from concrete; the dandelion cast as a weed. Uprooted from wherever they seems to grow. A tree that was meant to protect ends up soaking in all the sun. Still, the dandelion stands tall, sprouts yellow without the water. You feed your tulips or rose bush and it grows beautifully in your standards of beauty. But see the strength in the community that can turn trash into art. Can make flowers grow from concrete.

Kara Jackson

Chicago is the world's Harold's chicken box

open and picked apart
the heart of America that beats too fast,
because if you don't run quick enough,
you don't know who will shoot you.

In Chicago, the cops look like gargoyles with guns for teeth
the land of long buildings and lost boys. Sometimes I think
there is no name for Chicago,
just a mother's cry to the master of the earth
bring my baby home, speak up, bring my baby home
wherever he is, so I will breathe. For once.

Chicago is a rattling dashboard camera that fell off,
or broke, or maybe both.

The city of meticulous investigations,
where the people don't talk about death,
they just pull out everything from their pockets
and spread them on the table,
thinking *how much money can we bury a black boy in?*

The windy city where boys dangle and sway and spin and sputter
until the pavement feels better to sleep on than their own beds.

They can only sleep now.

Alfonzo Kahlil

When asked about Chicago
A confession

after Joshua Bennett

I've only been in New York a month
And I'm already used to the comments

Oh you from chicago?
I bet your favorite artist is Chief Keef
Wait, you drove here?
From Chiraq?
How'd you get out of there without a single bullet hole in your car?
Or yourself?

I'm sorry for your loss
In advance
If you haven't lost a homie by now, i'm sure you will

Give it time

Aren't you used to the color red by now?
What do you use, y'know, to get all the red from your clothes

And the cold sweat, you wake up with, from your brows?

I shrug them off
They don't understand

I just go back to my dorm / turn on the news

And note 12 people were shot in 7 hours back home

When asked about Chicago: an antidote

Don't ask me about Chicago
until you're prepared to hear
A love story

Krista Franklin

History, as Written by the Victors

The world is burning. Listen to Minnie Riperton on cassette tape. All of the records are in flames. The archives in ashes. Blood pools in the gutters of the streets. A black girl in a pair of '85 Air Jordans levitates down the block. She is clutching a copy of *The Red Record* she transcribed by hand, *The Book of Eli* in her backpack. All the buildings are boarded with eponymous red Xs on their Third Eyes. The house where Muddy Waters lived is broke down. Johnson Publishing is stripped and gutted like a woman of ill repute. The invisible fences between neighborhoods are electric. Howlin' Wolf is growling from the mouth of a seventeen-year-old on 71st Street squatting in the wreckage of Sun Ra's mothership, mumbling, *I'll feel better if you understand. You won't listen to me.* Black Youth Project 100 is holed up in an architectural effigy they psychically constructed of the house where Fred Hampton was murdered. A transgender fourteen-year-old in their ranks is finger-painting AfriCobra murals from memory on the walls with looted Kool-Aid packets and bottled water. A cluster of hooded teenagers is reciting lines from Gwendolyn Brooks poems in unison at the top of their lungs on the porch. *Remembering, with twinklings and twinges.* A freshly shorn Chief Keef speeds by on a dune buggy in a wasteland he created with his own hands. The North Side is surrounded by CPD in riot gear. White people there haven't seen the sun for decades.

This is Chicago as we know it, knew it, know it, knew it. Time is an illusion. Depending on the body that you live in, history is slippery as memory. All of it is a series of concentric circles. The question is where do we connect? And when? Imagine your mitochondria as a listing of names in a chattel slave ledger, or numerical assignment in an internment camp. Suppose your body a record of undocumented workers, or five generations of the spoils of war. Envision yourself booty, Loose Booty, walking the streets—the unholy offspring of poets and mass murderers, both colonized and colonizer intertwined in your cellular structure like an unpruned rose bush around a rotten trellis. What of history then? Think of the body—your body—as encyclopedic volume of one thousand years of experiences. In the middle of one book you have yet to crack exist facing pages, a story of the bludgeoned on one and the bludgeoner on the next. It's all one story: *The Book of the Dead, The Book of Life* nestled next to each other like sleeping children. They are dreaming dreams in your bloodstream.

Which side do you choose? What if you don't have to choose? These wormholes we call *History* and *Time* are the chronicle of near-biblical lies based on scientific fact. What happens if we wrap our arms around all of it? The Dead, the Living, the Soon Come, all the same time and space. The Good, the Bad, the Ugly, the Sinners and Saints, all inside us at this moment, right now. What if I looked you deep in your eyes and said, "You are the war-torn and the warmonger. Both the landlocked and the astronaut." And what does it matter? All of the history books are piled up and molding on the cold floor of a closed school anyway, and the average American couldn't tell you the top news story last week, much less comprehend the psychoociological importance of bringing down and burning every Confederate flag ever made and raised in this country. The room is divided between shoulder-shruggers and angry-faced emojis. God Bless America.

What we believe is this: The wasteland is the compost of the Now. The Future is already here, crawling, tottering like a drunk in the alleyways of time, walking like a sophisticate, running in the shadows with his pants slung low like a gunslinger. The final frontier is between your ears. It is postapocalyptic dystopia or utopic bliss depending on your position. We can stand in the sun or crouch wounded in the dark; regardless, it's all of our making.

We are major manifesters. Our DNA contains the skeletons in history's closet; our left foot is slave, our right is slave driver. These clouds of high-energy electrons are not static objects. Nothing is static. We exist in a continuum of time that is ever evolving, ever changing. We do not need to reinvent the wheel nor re-form the weapons. The moon and the sun go on playing an eternal game. We are natural phenomena engaged in an unhallowed battle with our mother. Time is not a line, it is a series of concentric circles. It is also an illusion constructed to induce us to consider the concept of progress as an intellectual exercise. Progress is a verb. The only universe we control is the one between our ears.

Our ancestors said, We shall not regard our swelled head as a sign of real glory, for shadows fade at evening. They asked us, ARE YOU LIGHT OR VERY DARK? We know that this is not an inquiry about flesh. We do not worry about history because we look into history's eyes when we brush our teeth in the morning. We flush streams of history down our toilets, throw chunks of it up when we drink too much gin. History digests our lunch. We blow history out of our nose. Even in this moment, history inhales and exhales, a secret agent and innocent bystander.

We believe that walls are witnesses. As are trees, and streetlamps lined along I-94. Even blue boxes, blind and blinking, carry our stories.

—*contains lines and phrases from Gwendolyn Brooks, Howlin' Wolf, Oliver Pitcher, Bob Kaufman, Aimé Césaire, Flavien Ranaivo, Wole Soyinka, and Winston Churchill*

Naudia j. Williams

Ye though I walk through Chi

Psalm 23 mashed with my life in Chicago

The CTA is my ride, I shall not walk.
It maketh me sit next to murderers of my kin and friends.
It leadeth me beside my grandma's lazy boy.
It restoreth my faith in my bus pass that works when it wants to.
It leadeth me home to my mother for her namesake.
Ye though I walk through the hood of Chicago
I shall fear no trap God.
For thou nina art with me
thy pepper spray and taser comfort me.
Thou preparest a table of Harold's
in the presence of my enemies.
Thou anointest my head with shea butter.
My fruit punch Arizona runneth over.
Surely flawless edges and Jordans shall follow me
all the days of my life and I will dwell
in a house of Englewood forever.

Jamila Woods
Ghazal for White Hen Pantry

beverly be the only south side you don't fit in
everybody in your neighborhood color of white hen

your brown bag tupperware lunch don't fill you
after school you cross the street, count quarters with white friends

you love 25¢ zebra cakes mom would never let you eat
you learn to white lie through white teeth at white hen

oreos in your palm, perm in your hair
everyone's irish in beverly, you just missin the white skin

pray they don't notice your burnt toast, unwondered bread
you be the brownest egg ever born from the white hen

pantry in your chest where you stuff all the Black in
distract from the syllables in your name with a white grin

keep your consonants crisp, your coffee milked, your hands visible
never touch the holiday painted windows of white hen

you made that mistake, scratched your initials in the paint
an unmarked crown victoria pulled up full of white men

they grabbed your wrist & wouldn't show you a badge
the manager clucked behind the counter, thick as a white hen

they told your friends to run home, but called the principal on you
& you learned Black sins cost much more than white ones

Sara Salgado

Holy Hermosa

On maps, the shape is graced by way of Bermuda Triangle
Fullerton; hyped-up wormhole when the streetlights go dead
thanks to the city's very own ComEd

Everything is combusted into neon,
it's all heated—keep it heavy, not healthy like carne asada stationary in your
    stomach over coke as you do bus-runs from Ashland west
the others think it's unexplored
but when you hit your stop, you better pull the cord
Kostner
praying grandma doesn't call you callejera

Can't mistake the coordinates con confusion
yes you may have visions gone pretty lucid
but your home isn't illusion

The crosswords of corners became a kaleidoscope I couldn't conquer
So it throbs still, sickly orange
you carry everything twisted from here

Next door, the landlord renews leases every year I got new neighbors
my latest cries on weekend nights asking Miguel to unlock the door
& she's sorry & she loves you & Miguel please open the damn door
nobody can sleep over your girlfriend's sobbing

On the other side of the block, where the sun meets the big yellow house
a chicken is roaming the lawn

Article in the Chicago Curb called it "the little hood west of Logan Square"
do not think we are a product of the young yuppies land wasted
you play the gentrification game, count hipsters past Pulaski
"why can't I come over" that's what everyone's been asking

Sun Times headlines
"Boy. 16. Shot in Hermosa Neighborhood"
"Boy. 16. Shot in Hermosa Neighborhood"

But hey, y'know Walt Disney was born here
too bad he took his American Dream come true with him

I'll bend you a new future Hermosa
the stories to justify your very name graced by Spanish prophecy
Beautiful
To make you whole,
finally.

Sammy Ortega

Corn man on every corner

The serenata of the elote man's horn
has the neighborhood
cha cha sliding into basements
for laundromat change.
White wood cart pushed
over potholes like uncalled for coffins.
Umbrella is shade
when the corn man traffics
clusters of corn in styrofoam.
Acres of unfertilized uncles
cropped out. I'm trying
to purchase him around the corner.
A dime bag passed around
47th and Halsted is a body
bag exchanged for liberation
money in Zacatecas, Mexico.
1 dollar on a stick.
2.25 in a cup.
After they kidnap kin
it's handed off. No napkin.
Ain't no negotiating
with the corn man.
My tio's
parmesan cheese fell
below my nail. That's why
I bite them so much.
A nickel will have my tio
back. Mama's been trying
to find pocket change
in the basement, her arms
are one dollar bills, always
WASHINGTONS. his salsa
valentina is trafficked down

your forearm. the elotero's
already cleared traffic on 47th St.
Louisiana hot sauce tear drop
for every uncle in a cup.
Chicago is someone's
unwatered lawn,
my homeland's cornfield.

Melinda Hernandez

Into a White Neighborhood

They look at me as if I'm a boarded up window
on a street that is half gentrified.
Limbs long like two empty lots on both sides of the house
I'm trying to embrace what I know:
hopscotch during sunsets
open fire hydrants on safe days
gun fire freeze tag
the water pipes are glue
jump rope in the night sky
attempt to catch the moon.

They see
wasps in the streetlights
scabies on God's skin
fruit flies in Hell's Kitchen.

We let our skin bake
in the culture of ancestors.
They come
tummies empty
mouths watering—
Mani-feast on our destiny.

Unpigmented homes plummet on Ridgeway
like nuclear bombs.
The ridge of our block
makes way for bread winners.
Suddenly, I'm the brown girl that made it
Into a White Neighborhood.

White neighborhood don't know
corner store walks
white socks turn a dingy gray.

White neighborhood don't know
I never asked for bleach
we're drowning in toxins.

White neighborhood don't know
mega mall is an art gallery.
White neighborhood see
mega mall as an urban outfitters
They pay forty dollars for a look we got for free.

Don't know we never needed a bloomingdale trail
Know damn well we can use the money to fund an education
Know damn well they're Jim Crowing our education.

I would have to be
1. My father must've left me as a child.
2. My parents had me at a young age.
3. My mom and dad both work double shifts to pay off the rent.

I'm never
4. The girl that got a 33 on her ACT.
5. The girl with a 4.7 GPA.
6. The girl who spends her summers writing with her peers.

And even if 1, 2, and 3 were true
followed by 4, 5, and 6,
I'd only be a glistening window
Robbing the light from the moon.
No one ever talks about the boarded up window
on a street that is half gentrified.

José Olivarez

Poem for Cal City
Confession

you were far south
but not South Side
what was i ashamed about

it's true   our school got locked down
the dogs sniffed through the halls
i said   whattup Folk

i thought it meant fam
maybe it does   it's true
John got shot   i didn't make it all up

i'm trying to remember
how it started   who started
calling you unsafe   calling

you a thug   my mom in her garden
a criminal   me in my books
gangster   John getting shot

in all my conversations   we were poor
not everything was a lie
facts were omitted

my brothers & i walking safely
to school   the cops searching
our lockers found mostly Pokemon cards

& weed   you weren't exactly hard
we were safe & loved
inexactly   John did get shot

it's true   he went to college
that's not a lie   he survived
so how come when i talk about home

it's smoke rising from the fire
of a gun   not the smoke
of fireworks   BBQs to toast

the new graduate

Natalie Rose Richardson

In the Bridgeport row house,

Chicago, IL

between the closing & opening shifts,
the boys roll spliffs with the same practiced
precision as shucking an oyster or unhooking a bra,
always talk of the stoned coworker who said
fuck it & did the unthinkable, always the hot girl,
the weed too weak, where'd the light go,
it's in your pocket, man; a *fuck that* cuts
smoke every few seconds, doors slammed
by visitors wanting to cop shit or sell it, & time
hangs still in its suspended blade.
Trevor cracks a joke about a *n-gger girl*, drags
the joint & passes it. You ought to be used to it,
the way these boys toss insults easily as they wake
in their skin, tuck unused Magnums in bed
-side drawers, never venture south of Pershing
except to pick up or make drops, shovel lines
of coke like tally marks for jail time bets.
But they are beautiful too, the boys—
lovely as flags hung from a window in breeze,
Everett who you once saw cry, his cheeks
flushed a dogwood kind of sunset,
B who wears his mother's ghost like a noose,
Kevin with his Irish teeth & cop uncle on trial
for shooting a Woodlawn boy, *bright fucking
daylight*—their how-you-beens, their girlish
eyelashes, their refrigerator bursting with Budweiser
& filets of snapper, their tongues imagining
the vacant lot of your hips, their chopping block
hands. They dream of owning a soul food restaurant,
wandering flea markets barefoot in India,
fucking with the lights on,
Irish whiskey, yards of kids, the Gulf's secret taste, daylight . . .

Michael Cuaresma

I'm from Chicago, but Not Really

"How exciting, a night out in the city? Maybe I'll find the love of my life downtown? He'll be tall, work downtown, dress nice, and is white. That goes without saying."

"Oh, of course."

"I say I'm from Chicago because it's easier than saying I'm from the suburbs."

"I take the Metra downtown every time with my friends."

"Chiraq is the best city ever."

"I don't understand why all those black people are rioting. Don't they know that violence doesn't solve anything?"

"Totally. Haven't they learned anything from Martin Luther King?"

"Why are they even protesting for Rahm to resign? He didn't shoot that black kid."

"Plus, didn't his parents get some million-dollar settlement anyways, before the video was released? Now they want money."

"Money from welfare, and money from their son's death. How fucking despicable."

"I thought you lived in the North Side? Why is your neighborhood so ghetto? At least you have a Starbucks."

"I love Lou Malnati's, but what's Harold's Chicken?"

"This homeless person sat next to me on the L and got off at the same stop as me. I pretended to be on the phone on my way back home."

"Why are people protesting instead of going to work and doing something? Like please stop complaining. My taxes pay enough."

"Go like my new profile picture. It's also on Instagram."

"Super cute!"

"Oh my god! I know, right? It's from the top of the John Hancock. Chicago is beautiful at night."

"I would totally live out like my twenties in the city, but I would never raise a family there."

"Same. I want my kids to have a normal childhood."

Claire DeRosa

Daughter

Every Friday my mother and I walk to the mosque
four blocks south, past the newsstand and a quick turn
from home. Some days I feel embarrassed to walk
the streets in my hijab and abaya. myself against
the skyscrapers, the glimmering city. Sometimes
I blush when strangers observe the fine stitching
my grandmother's arthritis-ridden hands created.

I am the girl who wears the white
prayer gown every Sunday to the mosque:
Isis, terrorism, hatred, guns fire, my neighbors
killed, bombs detonate all in the false names
of a religion that does not worship violence.

I am the girl without a heart.
They spit on the sidewalk at me
as if I am filthier than the minds
that raised them. Even the city
buildings I used to adore glare at me
Mock my distorted reflection
and say: I am a terrorist.

Pale faces swivel in my direction
Hands reach for palms of small children.

My dirty palms pray to Allah:

Do not look at the henna that reaches up my hand.
Do not stare at the hijab that brands me an outsider.
Do not linger on the brownness of my skin.
Look me straight in the eyes.
My traitorous eyes faded from prejudice.

I am a worshiper of a righteous Allah.

I am the daughter who loves to smile.
I am the girl in the white prayer gown.
I am a Muslim, proud to call this city home.

> *This poem is based on news events surrounding ISIS acts of terror, public testimonies of discrimination, and the experiences of people close to me. As a writer, I wanted to amplify people in our own communities in order to spread awareness and foster empathy, to build solidarity and break down hatred in a way that illustrates genuine resilience. I chose to use the first person to put both me and the reader in the character's shoes. However, it does not reflect my own direct real-life experiences.*

Gwendolyn Brooks College Prep Louder Than a Bomb Team

Damon

Damon is my brother
Damon is my friend
is my uncle
is my cousin

I remember how he pleaded with mama

I dont wanna go out there alone in englewood
Afraid to close both eyes in roseland

he picked up daddys gun.
No more running scared
with this sin in his hand.
safe passages were just
passages to his death
sentence. Soldiers
dropping dead
all over chiraq

somehow I felt gravity
was on his side like his
guinness skin could withstand
any bullet aimed

He could never be
A sacrifice. He could
never be hadiya
or trayvon cause
they were
regular kids.
(with red) I guess
just like him

I thought
the church
hymns and gospels
claiming the lord was
covering him in blood
would save him
(with Red)
I see the blood   now
covering the caps that lay
broken on the ground

Death be not bound to this cursed town

Death be not bound to my   brother

All he carried was a book bag
backpacked with ripened mind
now soiled dreams. All he carried
was a headset with rugged rap
that filled his ears till shots

it wasn't chief
keef this time

All he carried was a team full of brothers
Who didn't stand by him they ran

In squad we trust   amen

they fled like villains
that harbored dark
hearts disgusting
like the alley

the Chi: so timid in name
It's confusing how a city
with so much history is now
history for the boys playing
with guns buzz lightyears

and woodys making his story
end before it even has
a beginning

safe passages don't mean nothing
Darkness cannot push out darkness
only light can do that

when cops play with guns
and shoot somebody's son
instead of picking him up
piece by piece with peace
mending him, they've started
a cycle of repeated brokenness

And there was innocence before
They shot Damon dead
There was life before
this town put a death sentence
on our sons' heads
Chicago streets are lined with bombs
there are land mines out here
with the walking dead. Chicago
got so much soul but takes the hearts
of boys transitioning to men
who create gangs to replace families
(with green)

We pray these streets are streaked with god's hands
while we birth the devil to walk upon his sacred land
Soiled land. We're soiled man. Trying to cleanse
the streets with our brothers guinness skin
(with pink)

Trying to mend a city broken
by violence again and again
(with green)

Trying to find love
in the fear, our own hands.

It's confusing how a city with so much
history is now history for the boys
playing with guns

I don't want to go
out there alone

Raymesha Henry

Flatline

They can't relax
    because if it ain't about movin' packs
and packin' gats
it don't make sense.   Sense ain't so common
so common sense   a privilege to have
as a hustlin' black boy that watch his back
pack his gat and make sure his trigger finger
    on full attack. He makin'   sure to get gassed
up. try to go to school and pass, but cut
and don't nobody care enough
    to make sure lil homie   keep his grades   up.

ain't nobody at home.
    To make sure he ain't alone
and makin' sure he do no wrong,
        they all gone!
Mama fed up, she packed her shit
    and left.
Daddy followed the treble clef.
Brother sentenced to life in prison.
        He met death!
Sister liked gettin' doped up.
    sniffed coke up
    He said, "I'm out here, 'er day,   POSTED!"

He ain't know somebody else noticed

    lil homie still movin' those packs
packin' his gat, wit' his trigga finger on full attack
halfway watchin' his back,
    and lil homie
got some new connects,
    now he slang that crack!
Behind the scenes Big Folks watch his every move

60

waitin' for lil homie to snooze
        cause he know lil homie 'bout to lose
He gone make 'em choose   his life   or his money
clothes, and shoes.   On one of those slow days on the block:
no clucks buyin' rocks
        no niggas
                at the basketball court   chancin' shots
no chicken heads out to window shop.
                        he STOPS!
Cause shit get too quiet. . . .
        he hear a gun cock   a round of shots
so he pop back!
        Big folks determined to get lil homie packs
    his traps   and empty   his tech   in his back.
But lil homie ain't havin' that,   so he pop back!
Big folks finally get his gun cocked and back   at lil homie he shot
    three bullets caught 'em
                his vision started to crop   and his chest felt hot
    the quieter the shots.   Man   lil homie   got popped!

Aneko Jackson

Black Boy Dreams

What do you fear?
I fear dying at the hands of a man in a badge.
I fear the color of my skin will be the precursor to my inexistence
I fear that #BLACKLIVESDONTMATTER
and so far my theory has been proven true.
What's your fear?
I fear that boys gone keep dying for their dead homies & street names.
My black boy, why you gang bang?
Why you fear?
I fear cause my people dying.
Tired of family crying.
Tired of trying.
Trying to explain that this isn't culture
It's adaptation
I'm tired of our men having the same symptoms as war victims.
You blame us, but you built this damned system.
Only out of fear comes realization.
That where we live isn't choice
It's placement.
No More Fear
Cause one day we gone Bold Up.
Them liquor stores & churches ain't gone hold us.
Tell y'all, what y'all told us.
Be calm. Be peaceful.
But capitalism gotta die
like them black boys dreams do.

Anton Charles Sanders

Ode to North Lawndale

Damn. 12. The police. The Motherfucking CPD. Again I'm stopped for no reason, probably about to lose the rest of my day. I don't get it. As many NIG-GAS as there are in North Lawndale, I've unfortunately been chosen for one hundred lashes to my back. The only white people in my neighborhood are either the police or teachers. I hate that the only authority figures in my neighborhood are white. Shit, you could call North Lawndale its own plantation. That's probably what the slave owners of this generation think this is anyway. But what they don't know is, I'm planning an escape. I can't wait to be that runaway who comes back and saves his plantation.

CONTESTING THE NARRATIVE

Breanna Bonslater

Drill

Drill as in drill. as in gangsta rap. as in gun violence and trap house. Drill as in T-shirts with pictures on em saying "in loving memory." as in "free my nigga." Drill as in buildings made of brick, where dope dealers hide they bricks. Drill as in "don't come around here if you ain't from here." Drill as in thugs with pants being weighed down by gucci belts. as in gang violence and crack houses. as in the story of the people around me. Drill as in my uncle's life story. Drill as in what's happening on the streets. Drill as in the ugly truths. Drill as in my city's youth story. Drill as in the artist with beats that go hard, all these bars. Drill as in that Chicago style rap. as in that new generation gangsta rap. Drill as in the music that reminds me where home is.

Jake "Krez" Krzeczowski

Why Is the Chicago Police Department Targeting Chief Keef?

On June 17, moments after driving away from a courthouse in Skokie, Illinois, where he'd received a warning from a judge for a speeding arrest, Keith Cozart was stopped by two unmarked police cars. Brandishing automatic weapons, the officers ordered the seventeen-year-old to step out of his car and put him in handcuffs—this time for a misdemeanor trespassing charge.[1]

So far in 2013, almost one thousand people have been shot in Chicago. Almost two hundred have died as a result of their injuries. Both those numbers are sure to rise by the time this is published. The West and South Sides of the city, where most of the shootings occur, are frequently referred as "war zones." It is in this climate that two cars of South Side police officers made the hour-long drive north to suburban Skokie to stake out traffic court for Cozart, better known to the world as Chief Keef, arresting him for the third time in three months.

Since last year, when he blew up on the national hip-hop scene as a shirtless sixteen-year-old with a Kanye endorsement, Keef has been looked at as the face of violence in Chicago.

To be sure, the notoriety is not completely unwarranted. Keef, who refused to be interviewed for this story, watched his career take off from a couch at his grandmother's home while on house arrest for pointing a gun at a police officer.[2] He spent the first three months of 2013 at a youth prison in Chicago's west suburbs after an ill-advised interview at a gun range violated the terms of his parole.

The crimes are not so uncommon. The level of fame is. "A lot of the things these guys are going through now, I went through the same obstacles, but I was a little more mature about it and I wasn't famous," said Chicago artist King Louie. "He's not really into any violence, he just doesn't need to be in Chicago. He's not doing the violence but you definitely have to carry yourself a different way with the spotlight on you." For all the legal trouble Keef has encountered, only the charge of pointing a gun at an officer has been more than a misdemeanor, and that happened when he was fifteen. Other than that, it's been speeding, weed, trespassing. The police department's interest in him is starting to look like a "straw man" argument: build a character to resemble the larger problem and then knock him down. Knowing that it won't fix the larger problem but might grab them some positive PR.

These guys came all the way from the South Side to Skokie to pick him up for some warrant on a misdemeanor trespass.

Musicians have often been on the receiving end of this kind of treatment. In his 2010 memoir, *Life,* Keith Richards wrote, "Open season on the Stones had been declared since our last tour, the tour of '72, known as the STP. The State Department had noted riots (true), civil disobedience (also true), illicit sex (whatever that is), and violence across the United States. All the fault of us, mere minstrels."[3] After the Columbine shootings, Marilyn Manson came under fire for lyrics that were somehow supposed to have inspired Eric Harris and Dylan Klebold to murder their high school classmates—even though, as it turned out, they were not even fans. In this case, Keef is made out to be the biggest criminal in the city of Chicago.

"The media has basically been lying to the city and building up Chief Keef as the main person that is causing all the trouble," said Chicago producer Young Chop. "He is not in the streets like that, how they maybe used to be. It's crazy to me that media and police even think that way."

Chop has a point. Of the hundreds of killings, a total of zero have been attributed to Keef. There was the Lil JoJo incident, highly publicized as a Chicago hip-hop beef gone wrong, in which a fourteen-year-old aspiring artist was gunned down by gang members while riding his bike.[4] Speculation by major media outlets was that the murder stemmed from a diss-filled remix of Keef's "3hunna" by Jojo and his friends. Famously, stupidly, insensitively, Keef sent out a tweet saying "haha" after the killing. He was investigated by police for any possible involvement but never arrested.

Rather, Keef's arrests have been for petty offenses.

"These guys came all the way from the South Side to Skokie to pick him up for some warrant on a misdemeanor trespass," said Idris Peeda Pan, part of Keef's management team. "We're just pissed off. We're kind of like fed up at this point. We also found out recently that there's a task force of several officers assigned to strictly investigate our label, GBE, and its affiliates. Supposedly, to my knowledge, these are the same people that had something to do with arresting Lil Durk like a week or two ago."

The existence of the task force has not been substantiated by the CPD, who did not respond to phone calls and emails for this piece. We know that a similar operation was set up in New York during the last decade—much to the city's embarrassment.

Chicago's history of segregation along lines of race and class is well documented. A story as old as the city itself. In the 1940s, in a controversial, large-scale attempt at social engineering, the government started erecting low-income housing projects across the city, dotting the landscape with massive tenement buildings. In March 2011, with the experiment deemed a failure, the last of the high-rise tenements on the famously expensive "Gold Coast" on the city's northeast side fell to hungry real estate developers. Residents were pushed to the South and West Sides of the city and to suburbs like Englewood and Maywood—out of sight.

The city's history of pushing minorities and low-income families into increasingly inhospitable neighborhoods creates social problems that recreate themselves. This year the Chicago City Council approved the closing of over fifty schools, mostly in the city's South and West Sides.[5] The closings will cause students to travel farther to class, through perilous territory. Walking through unfamiliar gang turf to and from school poses a much larger danger to the youth of Chicago than a Chief Keef song. And with the city's newspapers failing, an argument can be made that rap artists are doing a better job of reporting on the story than anyone else.

"[There is] no doubt that in this day and time, violence is enforced by popular mainstream acts," said Chris Patterson, grant manager for Illinois governor Pat Quinn's Community Violence Prevention Program. "But on the flip side, those same acts are speaking out about injustices and [we're] not really seeing it for what it is. A lot of the perpetrators of these crimes are listeners who are poor and . . . under-educated by our so-called education system, which is letting them down in such a terrible way. If we are to pour our attention into anything, it should be rectifying the core or base conditions that lead one to rap about killing his brother or using excess amount of drugs—conditions such as getting them better schooling and housing."

Though thousands of guns are taken off the streets every year in Chicago, just as many flow right back into the city—most of them coming from the suburbs outside of Cook County, which have more relaxed gun laws. Gun owners are not required to report guns missing or stolen. To date this year, almost three thousand guns have been taken off the street, according to police superintendent Garry McCarthy and the CPD.

It's a subject that is not lost on the city's rap artists.

"They be shooting whether it's dark or not," says burgeoning star Chance the Rapper in his song "Paranoid." "I mean the days is pretty dark a lot / Down here it's easier to find a gun than it is to find a parking spot."

In an interview conducted earlier this year, he reiterated. "The accessibility to guns in Chicago is ridiculous," said Chance, who turned twenty this spring. "I can take you right now to get a gun for like $150. The fact that kids can get them is the fucked-up part—and music reflects people's ways of living."

A quick glance at recent CPD press releases shows just how deep and serious the problem of guns is in Chicago. On June 3 of this year, a nineteen-year-old convicted felon and gang member was arrested with a loaded machine gun in the Calumet district. Only minutes before, another gang member was picked up with a loaded .25 in Englewood.

On July 9, the Illinois state legislature voted in a statewide "concealed carry" law, allowing people to take loaded weapons into any business establishment that chooses to let them. Keith Cozart was fifteen years old when he was arrested with a gun.

Had Chief Keef come to national prominence through a crafty dance move or a corny marketing scheme, he probably wouldn't be facing the legal scrutiny he is today. But Keef burst into people's consciousness by rapping angrily about things he didn't like, shirtless, thrusting guns into a video camera. It's a disturbing image. Veteran Chicago rapper Lupe Fiasco said he was scared of Keef and his generation.[6]

To be sure, Keef is not a model citizen. He was arrested smoking marijuana in Atlanta a month ago, he was accused of being behind on child support payments, and he owns one of the most notorious and raunchy Instagram accounts around.[7]

For all his faults, though, it's hard to see how he deserves the treatment he has received from the CPD. And until the day he actually does something else seriously dangerous, their focus is probably better served by policing the part of the city widely known as "Chiraq."

"I really just think Keef has become a target at this point," says Andrew Barber of the popular Chicago hip-hop blog FakeShoreDrive. "Regardless of the content of his music, he's going to be pegged and singled out—it's just par for the course for him now. Does he bring some of the unwanted attention upon himself? Of course. But as with most rappers who've come from street backgrounds, once they see more of the world, their content, attitude, and actions change. Can Keef make this transition? Possibly. But he really needs to get out of Chicago, because people are just looking for excuses to bring him down."

The upper-class North Shore area might not be far enough away. There are rumblings from Keef's management that he may make a move to Los Angeles soon.

"The fact is a lot of people just know who Chief Keef is and are hating on him for just that reason," says Keef's friend and fellow Chicago rap artist Sasha Go Hard. "He's a legend. He's seventeen. He's on, he's getting money, and a lot of people just don't like the way he did that."

In a Vice documentary on Chicago's violence problem, South Side pastor and community activist Father Michael Pfleger of St. Sabina's voiced his opinion on the state of the city. "There has been a conscious decision to let some communities fall apart as long as it's contained and doesn't seep over," he said. "But guess what, America, it's seeping over."[8]

Chief Keef isn't so much a legitimate villain as he is an easy face to put to the violent environment he came from. To use Father Pfleger's example, Keef simply refused to be contained. If the arrest in Skokie last month is any indication, it is obvious the city is willing to do whatever is necessary to stop the seepage.

originally published in Complex Magazine, *July 31, 2013*

Notes

1. Chris Martins, "Chief Keef Served, Charged, and Arrested for Three Different Things in One Terrible Day," *Spin*, June 18, 2013, http://www.spin.com/articles/chief-keef-arrested-served-charged-courthouse-paternity-speeding.

2. Eric Diep, Daniel Troisi, and Sam Weiss, "South Side Story: A Chief Keef Timeline," *Complex*, December 18, 2012, http://www.complex.com/music/2012/11/chief-keef-timeline/chief-keef-is-arrested-by-chicago-police.

3. "Keith Richards Memoir, *Life*: The Speed Read," *Daily Beast*, October 27, 2010, http://www.thedailybeast.com/articles/2010/10/27/keith-richards-life-the-speed-read.html.

4. Lauren Nostro, "Chicago Rapper JoJo Releases Beef Video, Gets Killed, Twitter Reacts," *Complex*, September 5, 2012, http://www.complex.com/music/2012/09/chicago-rapper-jojo-releases-beef-video-gets-killed-twitter-reacts/.

5. Noreen S. Ahmed-Ullah, John Chase, and Bob Secter, "CPS Approves Largest School Closure in Chicago's History," *Chicago Tribune*, May 23, 2013, http://articles.chicagotribune.com/2013-05-23/news/chi-chicago-school-closings-20130522_1_chicago-teachers-union-byrd-bennett-one-high-school-program.

6. Daniel Isenberg, "Chief Keef Disses Lupe Fiasco on Twitter, Lupe Responds," *Complex*, September 5, 2012, http://www.complex.com/music/2012/09/chief-keef-disses-lupe-fiasco-on-twitter-lupe-responds.

7. Insanul Ahmed, "Apparently, Chief Keef Got Arrested Yesterday," *Complex*, May 21, 2013, http://www.complex.com/music/2013/05/chief-keef-arrested-atlanta.

8. "Chiraq: Global Gangsters," HBO, June 14, 2013, https://www.youtube.com/watch?v=5zn7BvKqTCY.

Kevin Coval

we real
January 2, 2013

The Glory Boys
on house arrest
at Grandma's

we real. we
steel. we
still here. we
no fear. we
know school lame. we
dope game. we
know gangs. we
Jeff Forte kids. we
jail bids. we
broke, bitch. we
capitalists. we
jupiter gassed. we
murdered fast. we
unseen we
wanting we
something we
more than one thing. we
eastside. we
southside. we
westside. we
on the block, we
high noon. you ravinia picnic and air condition. we
fire hydrant & fire, cracker. we
hot hell in June. you nap noon. you spoon. we
rap. we
die, soon

Demetrius Amparan

why do black boys smoke so much weed?

For those who keep asking

to simmer a blunt
deprive it of oxygen.

apply pressure to its blazing amber
until it burns no longer.

dangle it from your finger tips.
let the wind control its white smoke

forget about it for a while.

act like it knows your name.
pretend it knows how your god does.
ask if you'd shame your lord.

pass it to the ghost of your dead homie
let him inhale long enough to find closure.

cut loud
decibels of solace. wrap it
in the veins of your last odd.
hold it like your daughters hand.

suffocate it

with love.

tara c. mahadevan

Kill the Noise(y)

"We're in the Windy City—Chicago, home of deep dish pizza, the Bears, and the highest murder rate in America," Thomas Morton says plainly. He's the host of Noisey's 2014 eight-part documentary titled *Chiraq*, and that's the first thing he communicates: that Chicago—according to *Vice*, himself, and basically everyone—is known for its lawlessness; that the city is certainly befitting of the name "Chiraq."

Chiraq specifically focuses on the advent of drill music, and drill rapper Chief Keef and drill producer Young Chop's come-up—as well as other key figures in the genre, like Lil Durk and Fredo Santana—attempting to create some connective tissue between the subgenre and the city's segregation, crime, and socioeconomic disparities. Morton's opening statement is continued rhetoric in the Chiraq conversation, allowing the documentary to largely hinge on the cross-section of violence and drill music. And for them, the fabled, mythic creature that is Chief Keef sits at the center of it all. Keef doesn't say much in the series, but he doesn't have to: Morton speaks for him. He allows us to believe that Keef is exploitative in nature—that he began rapping to profit from it; that he knew his 2011 video for "Bang" would go viral, as if drill wasn't a genre that first had its own localized following before receiving national attention.

"I mean drill been going on, so it's like since Chicago hot, everybody just see [the violence]; people just be judgin' the shooting and all that. That stuff been going on before Chicago even got noticed with the drill music," drill rapper Katie Got Bandz says.

Her story is another large chunk that *Chiraq* misses, the documentary failing to mention any women of drill, particularly Katie, the designated Queen of Drill. Like Keef and Chop, Katie has a natural knack for rapping, using her Bronzeville neighborhood as her muse. For her, authenticity is paramount; she raps about what she sees. "I just basically tell my story, or talk about what's going on," she says. Rarely does she rap about people getting killed.

Vice and Morton warp the community's narrative in a way that best suits their needs. Only one episode is dedicated to a camp outside of drill, Vic Mensa and the SaveMoney crew, where Morton captures a moment when Mensa bails SaveMoney member Joey Purp out of jail. *Vice* pegs SaveMoney as something other than drill, but the episode doesn't offer any substantial facts about Mensa, Purp, or SaveMoney. Instead, Morton asks Mensa questions about drill music and drugs. The documentary glosses over these stories, presenting a disrespectful, misleading, and muddied viewpoint of a city rich in culture.

You might be asking why we're still talking about *Noisey's Chiraq* docuseries four years after it aired. The answer is simple: The media continues to make *Chiraq* relevant. In 2016, *Vice* released the forty-five-minute episode *Noisey: Chicago*, labeling it as a return to the city, but also as a way to make amends for *Chiraq's* negligence; *Noisey: Chicago* still clings to the same tunnel vision presented in *Chiraq*. Spike Lee also released his film *Chi-Raq* this past year, which, rather than presenting a positive path to pacifying Chicago's violence, instead makes a mockery of it. This is why the city fears outsiders. These pieces do a disservice to Chicago and have fetishized the city.

Indeed, Chicago rappers have celebrated their city as Chiraq, but outsiders have continually pushed the narrative; much like the lore that surrounds Keef, Chicago now has its own mythology. "At first, I used to say [Chiraq] until things started getting worse. Then I stopped saying I'm from Chiraq. I'm from Chicago," Katie says. "The violence been going on. . . . It's been like that. It just got worse once Chicago start being [big in] music."

For the last few years, the abuses of our justice system have been brought to the forefront, especially through the media. As the media attempts to show us the truth, and we become more aware of the racial inequalities that plague us, we see how heavy a hand the media really does have—and how the truth is skewed. When Michael Brown was gunned down in Ferguson, Missouri, in 2014, outlets like CNN fixated on almost purely inflammatory content: people in the streets burning cars and stores, people looting and pillaging. CNN rarely showed the peaceful protests, the people holding hands and holding signs in deference to Brown. CNN has even made this journalist distrustful of the media.

The media gains from this vitriolic narrative, using it to satiate the 24/7 news cycle. In Chicago, when a judge ordered the Chicago Police Department to release the tape of Laquan McDonald's death, a *Chicago Tribune* reporter tweeted an image of activist Malcolm London aggressively pushed up against some cops, his hand clenched in a fist in midair. London was quickly arrested and charged with aggravated battery to a police officer—not because of the photo—but it's these moments that the media (social media included) present to the public, helping to mold Chicago's image. What do these moments say about the city?

In May 2015, the outlet FiveThirtyEight published a study stating that while Chicago is one of the most diverse cities in America, it's also the most segregated city in America. Forget the diversity: it's the segregation, that negative arc, the public sees. The media—whether it's print newspapers, digital publications, television outlets, or TV and film—capitalize on Chicago's issues, which are systemic problems that affect the entire United States.

Chiraq, Noisey: Chicago, and *Chi-Raq* are problematic, reinforcing stigmas that the media and the world already embrace. And because of this media consumption, people don't want to get to know Chicago. The world concentrates on one portion of Chicago and villainizes it, when the city is flooded with talent—and there's so much else to see.

Musicians like Chance the Rapper and the band the Social Experiment have been bridging the gap between drill and Chicago's other rap circles. On Donnie Trumpet and SoX's album *Surf,* producer C-Sick—who has produced for King Louie and Fredo Santana—has writer credits on the cut "Warm Enough," while King L is featured on the track "Familiar." Chance has also worked with Young Chop, the designer of drill production. And Katie is creating more versatile music, working with Jeremih, Tyga, and Lil Debbie. Such collaborations by pillars of Chicago rap—a place disconnected not only by race but by neighborhood—help the city join together, and artistically unite the city.

As an outsider, I've felt my fair share of pushback from the Chicago hip-hop community—because Chicago is fearful of outsiders; because outsiders encouraged and advanced Chiraq. People have taken from the city for personal gain, disfiguring the community in the process. But Chicago has seen through the conflict that has historically separated the city and leveled it through music. By reaching out to musicians outside their respective crews, these artists are rewriting Chicago's narrative in the hopes that the world will see and take notice that something bigger is happening.

Nile Lansana

Windowpain
Raymond a.k.a. Lil' Ray

Sun don't shine too bright 'round here
Big brother tells me it glistens on the North Side
Window watching while sirens blaze
Turf in my toes
Sweet Baby Ray's
& chicken skin stain new white tee
Rust paints Jackson Pollock on calloused hands
Mama say these locks do the job, baby

I like listening to the silence
Bulls broadcast envelops the living room
Police car flutters past

Where
Moving trucks haul hollow hopes of escaping genocide
Politicians move like the wind
Chills on my nappy head in the coldest winter
Food deserts the Mayor overlooks while signing $5 million checks

Where
I constantly change velocity on walk home
Big Brother holds me close. he feels like
Something's boutta pop off
On the lookout like brothers lookin' for new kicks
Outfits organized by area
Not appearance

Purposeful dirt.
My slide tackles send opponents flying
Ugly dirt. Cement angel
Displayed on cold ground
Bystanders revel in bleeding silhouette

Beautiful dirt
When feet cultivate fire
Dig into soil/uncover history of juke & sweat
That footwork talk slick
Breathe of battle and breakbeat
& bop & bop & aye ayooooooo
A joy news don't cover
Movie never portray
When the strife make headlines
I just want to speak for the soul
Tell the truth about the "warzone"
I call home

The Land of the Misunderstood
Spike don't know nothin' bout my kingdom

Marwin "Stark of HUEY" Williams

The GO

Heads down, eyes closed, come and pray with me.
We took a hate city and made it a great city.
As much as it rains, it ain't hard to stay drippy.
And minimum wage went to 10 from 8.50.
Sometimes the wind makes my city cold.
Like, "How it's April and I'm still wearing winter clothes?"
But anyway, we all shine like we dipped in gold.
And all the women here badder than a six-year-old.
Knock-kneed, pigeon-toed. Back page, centerfold.
Either way, she hotter than a Uncle Remus dinner roll.

My dead homies went to the school of hard knocks.
They ain't dead; it's just the principal sent 'em home.
But I'ma see em again when school over.
Might have never been to the city, but you know us.
We ain't never shy; that's only a name.
And when Obama brought change, we started new culture.
Now I got angels surrounding me.
I'ma make my mama so proud of me.
Man, Flow too sears like the Tower.
Here we drop tapes and they sound like albums.
Trying to find peace, so I hide in the park where Barack from.
And Chance got us all feeling like we got one.

It ain't always pretty in my city,
but she make up for it when the weather hit the fifties.
Bopping like Diddy on the Dlow.
Trynna spread peace to my folks and my people.
Mild sauce on chicken and basement juke parties.
GCI playing your favorite new artists. Ohh.
They love saying that it's no love here.
But that's a lie cuz my daughter finna grow up here.
And I bet she be a Bulls fan, just like me.

This Chicago, nigga.
We don't trust Spike Lee.

Kevin Coval

notes for Mars Blackmon on the making of
Spike Lee's film *Chi-Raq*

- don't worry bout Kanye in the movie. ask King Louie
- him or Pacman coined *Chiraq* well before 2010
- the year Pacman was gunned down in Woodlawn
- drill. drillinois. the music of the automatic
- A-town snap turned Chicago halloween scene

do you know do you know do you know

- in the 90s, Mayor Daley went after the heads of gangs
- locked up chiefs and chefs and generals
- wiped out organizational infrastructure
- little ones started to wile out
- shootin like they was playing real life video games

it's gotta be the shoes

got to be pre-ordained
ordinanced and aldermaned
mathematically administered
prime numbers sinister

- you *can't* care what the mayor say
  cuz he don't live in the neighborhoods
  they talkin bout but he do close schools there.

- you *can* make the movie you want
  you sit courtside at the Knicks game. if you
  choose
  to do that shit, you got the stomach for any-
  thing.

• you *can't* believe the mayor care
        about each kid while ensuring only his own
        get safe passage and the best private education

• you *can* show the shit
        the city/country don't want the city/country
        to see. microscope the grand inequity

please baby please baby, baby baby please

• you been our main man since 1986
• good lookin gettin Rosie to dance to PE's *Fight the Power* like you did
• thank you for Buggin Out

no body no body no body

cover the faces.
the people who die
the people who live
here are real. in real
places that become
tropes for fear

• *you* can change that shit (at least a little bit)

the poet's job is to show
the auteurs' job is to show
the mother / father / family
face behind the statistics
that color the evening news
and reinforce the white
imagination

• put Durk, Herb, Sasha and Katie in there
• if you gonna work here / put folk to work here
• people too

the magazines say you gonna make a musical
based off a Greek comedy. ok, be careful though
cuz you still made Red Hook, still slanged
Js when kids were getting shot for them

- good lookin out on Bamboozled
- more shit like that please
- more 360° ballet majesties of the ingenuity of everyday people
- more Derrick Rose shooting at Murray Park
- more Team Englewood public high school poets practicing poems
- more culinary students at 63rd & Halsted cookin up the future

yo homes!

inflated/deflated
homes markets
marketeers
market tiers
show *that* shit
too

yo!

Mars Blackmon
the city segregated
like space is
from atmosphere
most fear
but you love
Brooklyn
and left it
for the upper
west side.

yo!

Mars

- love Chicago like you love Mike
- like you love his shoes
- and by his shoes i mean nike
- who made him mickey

Spike Lee
it is impossible to do the right thing
when america is wrong

we wish for something transformative
       • like when Little Richard made you Mike
       • and you could fly

you **can** do fly shit like that again

you **can** humanize half a city most the city/country refuse to see

you **can** give megaphone to the unheard, underfunded and under-

   resourced

you **can** point to the systemic historic white supremacist realities

       • why the name exists in the FIRST place

you **can** stop the onus placed on the shoulders of teenagers the city/coun-

   try has criminalized since bornday

you **can** help shift the public discourse

you **can** write some of this wrong by writing the real, Mars/Spike

you **can** do fly shit like that again

    please

    don't leave us

           hangin

A Nate Marshall Joint

Why I'm bootlegging *Chi-Raq*

When I saw the trailer of Spike Lee's forthcoming joint *Chi-Raq*, I felt vindicated. The film, borrowing its name from a pseudonym the city gained for its violent reputation, has been met with mixed enthusiasm. When it was announced earlier this year, people from City Hall to the hood questioned the naming of the film. City Hall wondered if it would be a film that damaged the city's tourism and commercial efforts. The hood wondered if it would it be a movie that trafficked in more of the same stereotypes and broad brushstrokes about what keeps black folks from being able to behave like decent people. The hood feared another story that positioned itself as an authority on how to fix without accounting for the nuances, histories, and divestments that created the conditions in these neighborhoods. I feared the unshakable corniness of a writer/director who hasn't put together a solid narrative film offering for the better part of a decade.

I can't for certain say what the movie does, but I can say I bet I'm right. I can also say that when it comes out, I'm bootlegging that joint, and I suggest you do the same for the following reasons:

1. The ham-fisted treatment of women in the story of Lysistrata brought into a contemporary context is concerning.

I understand the story of Lysistrata. I think it's an interesting and in some ways really brilliant example of classic Greek comedy. I also think it's some shit no man of this side of 300 B.C. should touch with the idea of a "repurposing." As an artist and as a hip-hop cat, I appreciate what it means to sample, repurpose, and reappropriate. Such notions are particularly important when we're talking about reimagining a canon for art that isn't limited to old dead cis straight white dudes. There has to be something subversive about the most notable Black director of all time taking this story and in doing so thumbing his nose at the pillars of Western civilization. Right?

Not really. Spike is, for his many positive attributes, still a man. That means he operates with the wind of an oppressive history in his sails when he makes a move that gestures toward. That means he can't really reclaim a sexist image and make it an empowering one, art be damned. Just like how I would have been super pressed if a white writer/director was the driving force behind the movie *Bamboozled*. Authorship matters and images matter. I don't see how this movie, given the premise and the trailer, avoids being yet another piece of art that builds its "edginess" at the expense of demeaning and dehumanizing Black women by reducing them to a series of organs that men want. I think a man at the helm of this film makes a difficult proposition an impossible one.

2. The dispossession of people's grief isn't an art project, it's cultural gentrification.

Spike Lee, more than many folks, should understand the trauma of gentrification. We've heard him talk about the wrong of newcomers to his home borough of Brooklyn feeling more entitled to their silence than committed to his father's cultural expression. How can he then feel more entitled to his commerce than committed to the real grief of real Chicagoans who are living in places where the violence is not a plot point? This disappoints me so much. People really feel the grief of losing a loved one or a neighbor in this city. People really feel the fear of being not far off from a similar fate. People feel the anger and frustration of helplessness as problems they did not create ravage their communities. I feel all those things. To consider those real feelings as a space for story development is erasure. It is building a luxury condo on the graves of Tyshawn and Hadiya and Derrion and countless others.

3. The opportunistic naming of this film is Willie Horton marketing.

Dog whistle promotion. Welfare queen advertising. This movie does not carry this name because it speaks to specific issues in the real places of Chicago that might constitute a Chi-Raq (that's not the whole city, ask any Chicagoan). This movie carries this name as a gimmick, a race baiting that trades on the public imagination's worst notions of what and who Black Chicago is. There might be some payoff to this (though I doubt it after seeing the trailer), but to this point it looks like a shameful and unironic publicity grab from an artist who should know better.

4. You can't have a conversation in good faith with a community you don't love, know, AND understand.

Spike, what's your favorite Harold's? What's your least favorite D Rose injury? What's the worst bus to take in the city? Who's your favorite high school basketball squad? Where's the best barbershop in the city? What's the best hood to get into some good trouble on a summer day? Who's your favorite House DJ? Where in Mississippi your people from?

I fear Spike Lee has forgotten the power of many of his early films. He was writing about people and communities that he knew and loved. He had insider knowledge of the history and context of those communities, and he brought that care and intellect to movies like *Do The Right Thing* or *School Daze*. To step into the narrative world of Chicago and assume either that you know what that means or that it doesn't matter that you don't is troubling and a betrayal of the genius of Spike Lee.

5. Seriously, Spike Lee making movies now is the film equivalent of late-career Dennis Rodman (or insert any over the hill once great figure who's now just kind of sad to watch).

Did y'all see *Da Sweet Blood of Jesus*? I'm not saying that it wasn't a gutsy move to remake a film with such a particularly strange storyline, but dang, Spike. The combination of bizarre story and jarring narrative decisions made for an utter fail. It's like a great player who is clearly past his prime and kind of sad. Clearly this is a dude who had game. Clearly this is one of the greats. Clearly this is a cat who needs some support that he just isn't getting. Clearly this is a train wreck. Clearly this is me watching my childhood favorite play himself into being a punchline.

The reason all of this troubles me is that I love Spike Lee. Despite everything. Despite an uneven catalog and his tendency to not listen, I love him. Despite rooting for a miserable franchise like the New York Knicks, I love him. I want to trust Spike Lee to tell an important, powerful story about my home, but I just can't right now. And I understand the major pitfall of writing this review-that's-not-even-a-review because I haven't seen this movie. I get it. I want to be generous to Spike Lee and to his demonstrated genius as an artist, so I'm reserving judgment on the movie in full. I'm just bringing up the mistakes that have already been made in the making and marketing of this film and pointing toward what those things might be symptoms of. I will still see the movie, and if it elevates the conversation in an unexpected way, I'll support it and encourage others to do so. But until I know it does that, I'm not giving any money to what seems to be a misguided mistelling from an outsider who should know better.

That's why I'm looking for a high quality bootleg. I want to have my faith restored, but until then, I'm not paying ten dollars for a movie downtown to have my hometown insulted. Now who got it for cheap?

THE CULTURE IS THE ART

Brooks Golden

(RIP FOREVER GOLDEN)

Alfonzo Kahlil

Rethinking Revolution
Creating Space for the Black Body through the Spoken Word

We know of course there's really no such thing as the "voiceless."
There are only the deliberately silenced, or the preferably unheard.
—ARUNDHATI ROY

It is 2008 in Chicago. Nate Marshall stands on a stage with nothing but his breath, his voice, and his body. This is no ordinary stage, though. This is Chicago's *Louder Than a Bomb* individual finals, a youth slam poetry event. Slam poetry is the act of reciting poetry out loud mixed with a performance of the body. In front of Marshall is a microphone to speak into and in front of that same microphone is an audience to listen to what he has to say. He begins his piece. *Look / I got these poets / shook!* It is not only his voice that lifts and moves. It is his body as well. He bobs and weaves, throws his hand in front of himself, and twitches his leg involuntarily with the rest of his limbs. His neck bulges with each word that propels from his mouth, revealing the emotion and intensity sitting behind the story he is trying to convey. He brags: *So come against me / it's essential that you'll lose / I'll leave your dreams deferred / my ego is Langston Huge.* Nate Marshall uses a rhyme cadence and diction that flow together, resembling a hip-hop artist rapping. In actuality, Nate Marshall is tapping into a history of performance poetry that has long been established by older political artists such as Gil Scott-Heron and the Black Arts Movement.

By all means, it is a beautiful performance of words and voice melding. By visual standards, it is very entertaining. However, like the black political poets that have come before Marshall, he writes from a personal narrative relating to his life. *Cause I'm a big bad gangsta cool kid who writes about his feelings / a mama's boy / a bastard child / a geek who has rapper style / a sensitive thug.* In that one line, from that poetry competition in 2008, we learn that Marshall is stereotyped as a gang member because of his personal interest in rap and hip-hop, but he has found a tool with which to shake his forced persona. Slam poetry. In that moment, Nate Marshall has *borne witness* and gained a platform, and therefore access to his own story. Using that platform, Marshall not only gains control of his own narrative, but he creates beauty and space through his sheer presence on the *Louder Than a Bomb* stage because it is not what is said, it is about who gets to say it.

In her essay "An Aesthetic of Blackness," bell hooks describes the need for the black body to create art and space and the conditions in which it develops naturally. Hooks details her grandmother's "ugly" home, where she learned how disenfranchised bodies are "shaped by space" and how they can give and take life due to the power spaces can possess (101). Hooks's grandmother differed from her parents, who were far more financially able. Hooks's grandmother lacked the financial stability to fill her life with resources and art and beauty, but she had access to items such as red peppers and lace curtains and she would hang them in her own home, her created space. Hooks's grandmother manufactured organic beauty from her everyday reality. Even in her grandmother's death, hooks muses, "Baba dies an old woman, out of place. Her funeral is also a place to see things, to recognize myself. How can I be sad in the face of death, surrounded by so much beauty. . . . We must learn to see" (101).

Through her grandmother's life, bell hooks poses an important question: What do you do, what does the black body do, with a history of lack of access to resources, beauty, and space? What is the black body's response to so much horror?

Nate Marshall stands on another stage in front of another audience. But he doesn't stay still for long. His begins his piece: *God Made The Hundreds, Man Made It Wild. them mama tell them / it wild over there / she say over there buses quit / running like utilities or resources / or dead boys.* This piece contains more personal narrative from Marshall's life. Marshall grew up in the Wild Hundreds, a neighborhood in Chicago known for its widespread poverty, numerous black bodies, and low resources among Chicago natives. He begins to dodge and weave, not like in a fight, but around the stage. Never staying in one spot for long, Marshall becomes a shark: the ability to stop moving is lost to him. The way he reads his writing, his cadence, comes out in staccato, choppy bursts.

His performance is reminiscent of a hip-hop performer, only with poetry instead of actual music. He continues to recount what he has borne witness to in his youth in this neighborhood: *in them hundreds / they schools / lock doors / after the tardy bell / like prison.*

Just as hooks's grandmother lacked and was actively blocked by scarce resources but created her own beauty through what she had access to, Marshall and other spoken-word artists do the same thing through what they have access to—their own bodies and voice. They do this through mediums such as stages like Chicago's youth spoken word event, *Louder Than a Bomb. LTAB* thus becomes the response to the disenfranchised black bodies' lack of space in Chicago. Kevin Coval, the co-creator of *LTAB*, has argued that spaces like *LTAB* provide a necessary space for black bodies with personal narratives, or bodies that have borne witness, in order to not only access their bodies and voice to create beauty through the spoken word, but to then use the stage as a platform to control their own narratives and a call to action.

"Louder Than a Bomb has emerged as a public pedagogy in order to hear many disparate voices in a radically segregated city and has served as tool to keep students in school in a failing public system where a freshman's chances of graduating are 50/50. This is the story of how and why the youth poetry work in Chicago exists, how it is transforming public cultural and educational space, and why what the young writers are saying is freshly imperative in affecting public discourse and why we must all listen to their poems" (Coval, "Louder Than a Bomb").

Essentially, these poems arise from hooks's theory that the need to create beauty and art is as necessary as food, shelter, water, clothing (102). And these poems need to be listened to because they point to problems in the communities of the black body, but these problems and disenfranchisement are recited from the black body's personal narrative and perspective. However, this method of creating space and beauty for the black body through spoken word does not come from nowhere, nor does it originate with Marshall. This is no coincidence. Nate Marshall is a breakbeat poet, a term coined and seemingly proclaimed by an older poet and playwright, Idris Goodwin, to describe the new generation of poets, from the 1980s to modern times, who intermingle hip-hop in their repertoire to make a political statement and bring about change in some form. Previous artists such as Public Enemy, Gil Scott-Heron, and the Last Poets have long since adopted this method of creating beauty through wordplay and spoken word. Add a beat to Marshall's performance and his lyrical diction and he would be indistinguishable from a hip-hop musician. *Lost Count: A Love Story* follows this form.

Nate Marshall and Demetrius Amparan stand on another stage. In front of these boys are microphones. In front of those microphones is an audience. It is May 25, 2009, and they are here at Brave New Voices, a national poetry competition, a bigger stage and a bigger platform than *LTAB*. They recite, they feel. Before they begin, names of victims who had died from urban violence in Chicago are read over a loudspeaker. During their performance, this voice will be their backdrop. It started before them and will persist after they themselves have left the stage. They begin in unison. *Will they ever call your death beautiful? Your life a sacrifice? Will the meeting of death and bullet ever be called romantic? A love story to be jealous of?* They crescendo and bellow in agony, *I'm 18, I play pickup basketball with ghosts.*

This is their story, and they just told it to a crowd of millions. They have used this platform as a call to action using only their bodies and their voices, while simultaneously accessing their bodies to create art from the everyday. They took what was regularly stereotyped and marginalized and made it into a work of art. This was an early work of Nate Marshall, created when he was a only a senior in high school. While he has his roots in the Chicago slam community, he was gaining recognition. However, this early performance is threaded throughout his current and future career because there is a common theme—the unrequited love of a city that seems to hate its citizens. The intermingling of grotesque hate and ebony love of the urban underbelly. This work in particular might seem contradictory. The overhead voice reciting the names implies tragedy, and the two boys performing the piece recount lament. How is this a love story? How can Chicago, its talons outstretched, ever hug a dark body and not leave streaks of red on its back? The significance comes in the form of a black body on stage, taking up space. That is where the real revolution lies.

Nate Marshall takes the stage again. He stands before a microphone. He begins his poem "Prelude": *he must've moved out / the neighborhood when i was little / when he was here i bet he could ball / probably could dunk / maybe he rap now.* Marshall continues to lament. He wears no smile upon his face; his face is not a mask, though. We see emotion cross his face, sometimes solemn, other times sad. We can see this is a personal topic for him. He mixes his performance with real events from his life: *i see it everywhere / RIP Pierre / RIP Bird / RIP D RIP Man Man.*

This stage has become a place to lay a body to rest, for Marshall's own story, own truth to come out. This is much what LTAB does. To tell one's own narrative from a sewn mouth.

Works Cited

hooks, bell. "An Aesthetic of Blackness: Strange and Oppositional." *Lenox Avenue* 1 (1995): 65–72.

Coval, Kevin. "Louder Than a Bomb: The Chicago Teen Poetry Festival and the Voices That Challenge and Change the Pedagogy of Class(room), Poetics, Place, and Space." In *Handbook of Public Pedagogy: Education and Learning beyond Schooling*, edited by Jennifer A. Sandlin, Brian D. Schultz, and Jake Burdick, 395–408. London: Routledge, 2010.

Coval, Kevin, Quraysh Ali Lansana, and Nate Marshall. *The BreakBeat Poets: New American Poetry in the Age of Hip-Hop*. Chicago: Haymarket Books, 2015.

Public Enemy. "Louder Than a Bomb." *Genius*, http://genius.com/4213202.

Marvin Tate

Hip-Hop Poet

Give us a poem that celebrates,
                                        struggles
cuts like a revolution that won,
that will sing at the top of its lungs, FREE AT LAST, FREE AT LAST,
THANK GAWWWDDDDDDDDDDDDDD'DAH ALMIGHTY,
dat we can see through all this BULLSHIT.
Somebody sample, in a *Black Kink Matter*
with Fela leading the way, blowing human-centric imagery
out of his sax, THIRD-WORLD LOVE, THIRD-WORLD LOVE!
Oppressed people going to be heard, don't care
if the 21st century is pre-recorded to look like Europe,
Brooklyn Heights, Portlandia, or the intersection of Milwaukee
& Damen Avenues. Spitting out words of wisdom like flying knives,
answers and their questions will be heard during the wine
and cheese segment of the program. Rescue Kanye;
drag him out from behind'dat window with dirty-knobs
he'll never be effective sitting down. Redefine blackness, the way Baraka,
Prince, Angela, Baldwin, and Missy did. Don't become frozen
   in time,
with *negritudeness*, *I'VE KNOWN RIVERS*,
                    I'VE KNOWN RIVERS, like a pick,
                    stuck in another lame-azz SLAM-
POEM. Acknowledge the world and its many colors and you will be immea-
   surable, Hip-Hop,
baby. In due time, in you will be dug by all,
saying shit like "Ya'know, dis'mo'fo is genius."
Elitist and intellectu'HOES will be forced to put down their guards about
what is ART and what ain't ART, like the mono-minded acting snobs they
   truly are,
while you return to the hood. YOU, with your three-foot head of dreads
   and JuJu beads.
                    YOU'ah, inner-city buzzword now,
                                        a breath of fresh air,

a Hip-Hop Poet,

a real family.

Nate Marshall

Woop Wop De Bam

by the time you get this transmission
we'll already be off this planet
or on the bus heading downtown
scratch bombing our last will & testament
into some commuter's view. here's the thing:

everything you don't know is intentional.
either by you or by us. don't act like you mad
you can't hear the words we radio edited out.
you remember that scene in white men can't jump
when the question of listening & hearing is raised.

you knew then that there could be nothing between us
except rhythmic static. you know our whole dialect
is a raw hide stretched into a handclap, a record scratch,
a jive so unintelligible it must be genius.
you seen us leaning against the whole world with one foot up,
cocked back like a prayer.

you seen us in your corporate offices. creeping in black
as something black & live. we know your slang too.
better than you. we invented that & gave it to you
for whatever winter equinox holiday you prefer.
we know african-american is how you say nigger in a board room.

we're hip to your myriad of words for desertion or starvation or genocide.
even our conversation filler is a conjuring. the dark cousin
of your *whatchamacallit* & *thingamajig*.
our whole steez a code you can't break, can't even dent,
can't fade in the least & we see you finna try.

KZ

Search

When you google spoken word / is the first post about sadness or blackness /
    am I being redundant //

When you google spoken word / is it of mental illness / poverty and mental
    illness / labeled 'illegal' and sad / mentally illegally brown // or

When you google spoken word
do the top hits become crystal ball
a conjuring up of whitewashed train line boundary
 newly renovated
a building up of better Chicago

                                         a cleaning out
a Wicker Park watering hole / host of hipster feeding frenzy

See
    that's the thing about being drunk / all the things start to out of order
        get / start to get order out of //
a weathered westside pothole
a desire of functioning out of queer feminist yoda-ing

See
    that's the thing about being black / sad / drunk. more often than not / or
      labeled ill-femme-mentally black / the terms all start to merge

The top hits should be Chicago heart / and its extremities / am I being
    redundant //
a collective of extreme south Hundreds / west K Town / north Rogers //
      never the center

a collective of color //
      that's never centered

Something about midwestern smack / sadness / about police / hopelessness //
   or

brown bodies in the streets stopping traffic / delaying flights / making
   speeches for other black people / about hopefulness //
in Chicago / they are the same thing

that's the sobering fact of Chicago violence / and action
they make you want to be an activist / writer / of spoken word // perhaps

When you google it / I hope you find //

                                           its real veins

Jalen Kobayashi

The Stoop

after Gordon Parks & Ralph Ellison

Chicago-Nowhere

Shhhh . . . I go nowhere.

we be on the corner like a lamppost.
posted up on the block/ postman
post to be in school

This stoop, a manhole
covers the X marking
the spot under an awning.
rolling dice until morning.
clouds rolling in, the ol heads
rolling blunts.

The Stoop is a commonwealth
Of Blue and Black.
every greeting a 3 finger flutter
and a snap.

The Stoop, a checkpoint
for aliens 6 blocks away
coming to see cousins
And run their pockets
now we are rolling

Chicago don't wear nothing
but bulletproof. it's never ending
summer for my friends.
we all take turns on The Stoop.

this is a podium
for the youngest child of 6
for the food stamps and WIC
for the boarded up and broken bricked

Casting a spell.
Jail hold a casting call.
Soon as responsibility hold one we disappear like casper.
We spreading in the city like cancer.
We are the cancer paper and the mouth piece

Corner store concoctions
takis and arizona
make their way here
(6 deep)
who needs an X-Box/hoverboard/basketball rim
when you have the stoop

none of us live
here
neighbors use sprinklers
to deflect our daily rendezvous.
Our pockets never dry

when we are on this stoop
we wait for the next to arrive
Roll up.
in minivans,
We get smoked
            Out
siblings in the back
beg for their rotation
on the stoop

this stoop is Chicago
one block from the Ave
I go. Nowhere.
this stoop is a stale sandcastle
unnaturally holding its place

this stoop be
super donuts
and
school buses
free lunches
and prenup

we stay
over here, occasionally go
to the court, always
bailing

others take over our stoop
no neighborhood
watch
badge, instead a branding on their hands
and brandy in their hands
bandannas straining syllables through cloth

a barrage of bullets is proof
we must continue walking.

KZ

Slay

when white girls speak Chicago slang
> ~ I picture them a creature of the night ~ a crawling thing ~ they come
> out from under the beds of colored girls ~ chew them up ~ swallow
> them whole ~ each time she speaks a piece of colored limb is escap-
> ing its cage in her ribs
>
> ~ Colored lips are *Yasss Gurh* ~ the naps at the back of her head
> are *Werk* ~ *On Fleek,* the bite of her cheekbones ~ Colored
> backbone is *Squad* ~ when she say *It's Lit,* it is a black girl's soul
> set aflame ~ a summoning forth of all her fire
>
> ~ Pieces of Colored girl climb out of her mouth ~ reassemble
> themselves into soldier

the White Girl will say
> "You judge too quickly. always pining at the thought of my
> demise. you try being a body with no organs. bones without the
> meat. they will think you a carcass. the picked over remains of the
> meal. you never wonder at why birds chirp at midnight these days?
> at why the stars have always swallowed up blackness? yaaas gurh.
> you need me. you try creating culture from nothing. you try
> making fire without wood. being the dam to all that water. holding
> back all that power. and you'd deem me racist for liking it dark
> when it is night outside?

and Colored Girl will say
> "I have done all this and more. You talk of stars as if you know
> what it means to be solar powered. You try holding the sun inside
> your chest without Icarus's whisper in your ear. I *have* thought of
> why the birds sing at midnight. in fact it must mean there is a
> change coming in the winds. a shift in power. the seasons too.
> Once cold months take summer's form now. which is to say that
> the last shall be first and the first shall be last. which is to say that
> colored girls are redefining the phoenix."

as Colored Girl speaks
    I imagine her volcanoing out of translucent sunburned skin and
        blue veins. A dawning from her own unending night. A taking
        back of the underside of her mattress.
    She says "We coolin'" and White Girl rechecks the Urban
        Dictionary tab at the base of her neck. Colored girl slices skulls off
        of White Girls' hydra heads. unbothered. by the way they grow
        back.
    Say, "Look, you decent, but you tweakin if you think I still fuck
        witchu." White Girl's tongue is stranded inside herself. In perpetual
        yoga sphinx pose. White Girl trembles, cries out for Iggy and
        Colored Girl says "Shit, it's been a minute since I did this, but I
        could slay you all night. slide on over Ion't give a fuck about these
        sheets, nigga shit my bedroom would look better when I paint it
        with you. Bet."
    Colored Girl slays the kraken from inside its belly, which is to say
        that Jonah could've used a colored girl out on that water
    White Girl screams, melts into the sticky underpart of Colored
        Girl's heel. Colored Girl says "Where yo chill at?" and relearns
        who her body is, unbound.

White Girl is medusa head turned stone
boogeyman shadow
she whispers now, with permanently lost voice
            with a trachea ripped ragged from Colored Girl's unleashed limbs
The last piece of Colored Girl jumps off of White Girl's lips
Colored Girl's middle finger, the final "Slayyyyy, bitch" a reminder
                                that colored girls slay

        monsters :
                            : even the ones they reside

        in

E'mon Lauren

Speak

i got a family reunion in my mouth. chuuch under my tongue. loud packed loose squared language. bootlegged babble. mild saucy and slick. quick card crackin gramma. squad a sanctuary on my top lip. throw the handles of my cheeks. what's good in the hood of your mouth? the yo in my yawn. a fugase flap/flick of tongue. southside schtick slobbered. a candy lady's cabinet. bud and MC lite/Lyte a boombox on my beak. suited and booted. food and liquor leaking. tripping on my tonsil. a(1/k47). the rink skating on my *no*'s and what consent mean. my gots belong to Giovanni and Jasmine. a different world in a dutch masters. elbows off the table of my teeth. don't you have any manners. melanin in the suck. Auntie Pokie neck roll caught in my throat. i speak a queer language. color coded. no code switch or swap in my mouth. i hold a rainbow coalition on my tongue. obama care in my back throat. let my Mom claim the baby in my teeth for tax season. i speak sacrifice. urban dictionary in the suburbs. know my rights and speak them. loud. like my music. like my body. like my bossy. i speak my bossy. i speak Trina and Cardi B. i speak woman runs the house. i speak field and house. i speak house. chicago. chicagu. chic a go. redline lingering lick. i speak shaa(r)p. sharp sword. bible translations. revenue. avenues and blvds. stomping grounds when i chew. cabrini mouths Moms greens. leclaire courts on 26th and california. i speak free my mans. i speak free my energy. i speak in royalist. in concrete king/queendoms.

Sammy Ortega

I TAG CTA

Chicago Transit
Author not Authority
I make neighbors with insufficient fare
Put their hands against the wall
Their stories tagged in oink ink
Makes them authors
Now they ain't insufficient
Now they earned fare
Now they created jobs
CTA custodians are paid by the hour
To clean graffiti
It's reading a Chicago native story
Then erasing it
The Nina and the Pinta are
Express trains
Headed towards Western
Orange line
You can't say we didn't
Create a workplace with
Higher demand

Leah Love

Flower Breaking through the Concrete
An Interview with Liz Lazdins

"Like so many young people, I felt invincible."

At around age sixteen, Liz Lazdins (aka Beloved, aka Liz1) took to painting graffiti (graf) in her native Hyde Park with zero hesitations. "I saw guys from the neighborhood getting their names up and I wanted to too," she says. Since then, Lazdins has become a prolific artist and activist around Chicago, co-founding Vision Village, painting murals, and curating art shows. Weeks after the close of her the show at the Hyde Park Arts Center, we spoke about fears, hip-hop, and of course, art.

What did you do before tagging?

Before tagging, I was a kid doing kid stuff. Going to school and hanging with my friends in the park. I was mischievous, but I would not say a troublemaker. Around the time, I got into graf others started getting into drinking, parties, and drugs. I went to hip-hop parties, but my vices were rapping and bombing.

What is it like being a female tagger? Is it easier now? Was it ever difficult?

Being in a male-dominated scene did have difficulties, but there are more women in the game now. Women are more accepted within the subculture. I was fortunate that I had positive and supportive guys who gave me respect. The good thing about an intense activity like graf is that if you have skills you will eventually get respect. That is why it is so important now that women are more accepted on the scene and that they develop their skills. I am hoping to someday hear of an all-city *female* king of the city, someone who is consistently up on all train lines in the city.

In terms of violence, how has the scene changed since you started?

I am not a teen anymore. I am not on the trains and the buses every day anymore. I take my kids to school, paint when I can, and don't go out much (sleep! precious sleep!). I think the graf scene is still a safe haven for youth trying to stay away from gangs. However, out of all the facets of hip-hop, graf is the most dangerous. Graffiti writers can get territorial and fight more than rappers. As I understand it, graf is nothing compared to gang life. When I was coming up, we made a point to use rap, dance, DJing, and graf as a way to compete with each other (battle) rather than fight. Most of the time it worked. The youth of today are smart, as we were, and I am sure they have these and even more outlets. Of course, those of us on the outside only hear about the bad stuff. All people are exposed to violence, dehumanization, and sexualization. We are living in a constant state of war overseas and in the streets. All that is even more severe than when I was a teen. I pray for those coming up not to drink the Kool-Aid, and see the brainwashing and fake "American Dream" for what they are—a distraction to keep them from being free and loving each other.

What is your greatest fear as a public artist?

All artists who engage in illegal activities worry about arrest. The real shame is the overcriminalization of graf and street art. Compared to what many urban youth could get into, graf is tame and nonviolent. Cities all over the world have embraced graf and street art—Barcelona, São Paulo, and Berlin, etc. It fills the streets with color and soul. It is ironic that the country that originated style writing with spray paint on trains is so slow to embrace it. Most likely that is because of who originated it—lower-income brown-skinned urban youth. Now we see, as with many grassroots movements, the appropriation of the letter styles, spray styles by corporations and media. We even see buses and trains wrapped with ads where our colorful tags and pieces used to be!

What exactly is people's beef with graffiti?

That depends on the person. Owners feel violated if someone writes on their private property. Companies feel their authority questioned when their billboards or buses are painted on. Politicians and cops worry that it will look like they do not control their city. Regular folks get frustrated because they do not understand what the graffitist is saying. Mostly it is the idea that not everything can be controlled that stresses out the capitalists and government agencies. If graffiti writers and artists were given the freedom to create, most regular people would love all the beautiful artwork in dead spaces that they could see free: the People's Art Museum.

Is it a challenge to balance your roles as both an activist and an artist?

Not at all. Social justice inspires my art, and I hope my art inspires people to continue struggling for a better future. The issues appear naturally in my pieces because they are so much a part of my thoughts and the lives of those I am inspired to draw.

Back in the day, you helped found Vision Village, a hip-hop community center. How did that happen and what was your role in it?

A few of us rented a huge basement space. We lived in the side rooms and used the common space for activities. It started with Upski, Lunchbox from Stony Island, photographer Morgan Pruitt, and myself. Artists like Stu from J. Davis Trio, The Brickheadz, Stef Skillz, Tree Roots, Ang 13, Lavie Raven, Dmnology, and so many others passed through the space to work on projects, crash, or get a meal. The best were the rhyme sessions where we would just play, beat, and write verses together. Oh, the freestyle sessions! We did not play around back then in the rhyme cypher—it was a very intense spiritual thing.

Can you elaborate?

We held drawing and writing groups, played chess, breakdance practice, women's art show, and workshops. It was all very organic—a space for us to do our thing—there were no after school hip-hop programs then. Music venues and art galleries, for the most part, were not trying to deal with us—a bunch of crazy street kids and young adults! It was crazy too. We wanted to be rebels— have no structure—but we quickly learned that work is not done that way and no one wants to do the dishes. The Village only lasted about two years, but it was a creative space for many.

What kind of activist work have you been doing recently?

Lately, I have been less on the activist scene—I am recently married and rais- ing two kids. I always try to think like an activist. For me, this means engaging in conversations with friends and family about current events like Ferguson, the drone bombings in Yemen, or the water in Flint. I also try to attend events that people organize or at least promote them because I know organizing teach-ins or rallies is work usually done by a few dedicated people. The very least the rest of us who want change could do is show up, learn something, and incorporate it into our homes or neighborhoods.

You cannot live on the South Side and not talk about the violence in the city. Since my early teens, I have been schooled by elders and witnessed white privilege in action, racist cops, and the uneven distribution of resources throughout the city. I spend time thinking about my own role in it all. For instance, I would love to paint murals in Englewood paying tribute to the community or beautifying the wall, but in a way, I think it is inappropriate for a white girl to be over there painting their walls when there are probably plenty of amazing local black artists. I am undecided.

With graffiti, some of the appeal is about being able to make the city your own. Do you feel that?

Absolutely. When you feel you have no voice, no power putting your name up for the world to see, it feels good. Many might see the act as an illusion—a meaningless gesture—but actually, a good graffiti writer knows the city better than 99 percent of us. They know where construction is happening; they know how to climb buildings, all the alleys, bus routes, when cops come on and off shift. Some even know how to run the train tunnels to get from one end of downtown to the other. They know all the quiet secret spots under bridges, through vacant lots, and on freight tracks. In addition, because writers often hook up from different neighborhoods, they know more than their areas. Sure, they do not actually own anything, but the knowledge is empowering and useful.

Kane One

in the business
a manifesto

Hello my name is Miguel Aguilar, or in oppressive dialect Meegwell Agweelar.

I am not a poet.

These days I am calling myself an urban philanthropist.

Today, I have some images, and I have some thoughts.

I'm in the business of people.

I'm in the business of people convening.

I'm in the business of people convening for the sake of loving each other.

I'm in the business of people convening for the sake of loving each other before and while systems and formats attempt to keep them in isolation.

You don't need a permanent address to love.

You don't need to sign a liability waiver to love.

You don't need to take the bus 3 miles to a library that has internet in order to fill out an online application and set up a free gmail account to hit a verification link in order to love.

You can love the other 14 people in a jail cell with you for the next 23 hours and 59 seconds.

You can love across gang borders and race borders and gender binaries and computer operating systems.

I'm in the business of restoring ourselves from before and beyond the white gaze.

I'm in the business of hearing Delfonics songs in my head while lily white ladies lecture me on how my work isn't what they were expecting and still need for me to do even more work by unpacking it for them even further.

I'm in the business of reminding our black & brown children that graffiti and public space are still ours, no matter how many white artists with formal training have thousands of Instagram followers and camera crews and tv shows and large scale commissions on downtown buildings.

I'm in the business of carving out and preserving spaces that white people have a hard time finding out about, because they will always inevitably find out.

I'm in the business of telling white academia to wait patiently in the hallway until we are done cooking and improvising and singing and dancing and exhausting all possibilities.

Until we are ready for you to come and devour our latest iteration of culture and magic.

Leah Love

On Afrofuturism
A Roundtable Discussion with D. Denenge Akpem, Damon Locks, and Ytasha L. Womack

The future is unpredictable. In the world we live in, in this city, sometimes it takes everything you have to survive in the present, never mind worrying about the decades ahead. Afrofuturism is a beacon of light in our darkened edifice. What Afrofuturism is exactly depends on whom you ask, but broadly, it is the future from the perspective of African Americans. It surprised me to learn that this aesthetic movement has a home in Chicago. In retrospect, however, it is not surprising that the same people who turned a bitter, leafy vegetable into a cultural staple also managed to transform fears and dreams of the future into artistic representation. To find out more about Afrofuturism in the time of "Chiraq" I talked to three Chicago-based creatives.

D. Denenge Akpem is a an Afrofuturist space sculptor, performance artist, designer, writer, and educator whose work connects site-specific sculpture, ritual, public art practice, interior design, and science fiction. Born in Nigeria, Akpem is the creator and teacher of "Afrofuturism: Pathways to Black Liberation," the first course of its kind. She is the founder of Denenge Design+ Studio Verto and is a lecturer at the School of the Art Institute of Chicago and faculty at Columbia College Chicago.

Damon Locks is a musician and visual artist. A founding member of the band Trenchmouth, Locks has worked with the Center for Urban Pedagogy and has created art for IFC's *Portlandia* and films such as *The Interrupters*. His intricate artwork spans mediums, and he is a teaching artist for the Prison + Neighborhood Arts Project.

Ytasha L. Womack is an author, filmmaker, futurist, and dancer. Her book *Afrofuturism: The World of Black Sci Fi and Fantasy* is a 2014 Locus Award Finalist in the nonfiction category. In addition, she has written *Rayla 2212* and *Post Black: How a New Generation Is Redefining African American Identity*, and has written and directed the films *Love Shorts*, *The Engagement*, and *Bar Star City*.

✳

As teachers, artists, and writers, how do you define and think about Afrofuturism?

Ytasha L. Womack: Afrofuturism is a way of looking at the future or alternate realities through a black cultural lens. It is an intersection between black culture, the imagination, technology, liberation, and mysticism. Afrofuturism functions as an artistic aesthetic, method of self-liberation, healing, and a basis for critical race theory.

Damon Locks: I think about my intentions. What moves me. I am not particularly interested in categories. I feel people often couch similarities, or look for connections, to create or control a history after work is done. I am less interested in stepping into categories and viewing my own work within parameters. Asking questions is much more interesting than having an answer. We are writing the sentence. The name of the category is like a period at the end of the sentence. I don't want to write the period before I finish my sentence. People like Sun Ra, George Clinton, and Lee Scratch Perry were all black people making work and doing their thing. They all were a part of the African diaspora. They all pulled from their inherited cultural and contemporary culture to build new work because of how their individual minds interpreted the raw materials.

D. Denenge Akpem: It is important to me to show the range and breadth of artists related to this field but also not to impose the category of "Afrofuturism" on them. I always qualify, and in their media projects, students need to answer the question of whether the artists they are focusing on have themselves adopted or rejected that category. There is contention around the term "Afrofuturism," too, and I respect any terms that people wish to use to describe this genre. Although some people take issue with that, a white man, scholar Mark Dery, coined the term "Afrofuturism." For me, I connect it to Malcolm X's use of "Afro-American" and to Mark Rockeymoore's fantastic metaphor of the Afro in connection with the field as something that spirals out and cannot be contained. It is in homage to Rockeymoore's description in the essay "What Is Afrofuturism?" that I continue to reference this term.[1] Some people erroneously see Afrofuturism as all about wanting to go to outer space. Yes, that is a part of it, but for me, it is about Black liberation. Moreover, that starts/exists here on Earth. It is about love for Earth, self, communities, and future.

What about Chicago attracts Afrofuturist-leaning artists here?

Y.L.L.: Chicago has an established history of activism, organizing, art, and music. Chicago's culture stands apart from other cities. It is very much a mix of big city and a small town. There is much overlap of communities within black culture in the city. Dissecting blackness and ideologies is a pastime here, which makes for a fascinating backdrop. There is a lot of conversation about the future, and change is due to the nature of politics in Chicago.

D.D.A.: Chicago is also an incredible site of artistic production that spans generations. There is something about this city. . . . Chicago was the home of Sun Ra, his papers, and so many musicians, artists worked and were inspired by him. There is a dedicated group of Afro-Futurists who keep this liberatory Afrofuturist vision alive here, which is why the genre is connected to this city. There are many black women artists here who have been engaged with Afrofuturism for quite some time in terms of contemporary art. We need to be aware and honor the ongoing work that goes into Afrofuturist practices. This does not just happen; it is intentional.

What is your personal vision for the future, and what does liberation look like to you?

D.D.A.: Science fiction has always helped me to find myself, an avenue of liberation especially when I found myself in untenable situations. This is foundational to my approach to Afrofuturism, which I see as a methodology of empowerment, a source of inspiration, and a way of sculpting the future. Ourselves, our bodies, the spaces we occupy, the world around us: all can be reshaped in a conscious and decolonized manner. I believe this, and it is space for this kind of power that I create in the courses I teach on Afrofuturism and Black Arts.

Y.L.L.: As a storyteller, I think it's important to have the ability to tell stories and connect with your audience. This sounds simple, but until fairly recently, it wasn't always easy for people of color to get works out. Technology has made it easier in many ways to get stories and perspectives out to the world. Liberation is being able to tell your own story. Liberation is being able to live the life you want (as long as you aren't hurting people) and to be able to learn what you need to learn to make that happen.

How does the present compare to the futures you may have imagined as a kid?

Y.L.L.: In many ways the present reflects the future I imagined. We have an African American president and I am able to communicate with people everywhere all the time via the Internet. We take this for granted now, but these ideas were forward thinking a few years ago. I didn't think we'd still be engaged in war as a way of settling disputes. I thought there would be more sensitivity and supports for mental health—maybe there are more, just not enough. I also thought gun violence would be minimized.

D.L.: I have always been dystopic. Things like *Blade Runner* and *Escape from New York* informed my visions of the future, as a child. I stay cynical. I do the best I can.

D.D.A.: The present is the reality of being an adult and having to take care of "adult" things like rent, nourishment, and transportation. It is the reality of being black and a woman living in the USA. I have to prioritize self-care in all its forms because if we don't take care of ourselves, who will? If we don't stand up for ourselves, who will? I work to build networks and relationships, strands and tentacles of connection across diverse groups, even as I require a lot of solitary time to complete work. As a child, I didn't spend a lot of time thinking about the future; I was present focused. The one major thing I did dream about, though, after a visit to Chicago and seeing Bertrand Goldberg's Marina City Towers, was moving there and having a flying car to dock on the balcony. However, flying cars for regular everyday use have not transpired yet, and I have yet to move to Marina City. In my imagination, I was going to be living a much more Jetsons-style existence, including orbiting Earth in a space hotel for a spa weekend.

Is there anything in particular that you have enjoyed recently? Moreover, what were you into, media-wise, when you were a kid? How did it influence you, as an artist and as a person?

Y.L.L.: I enjoy reading science books, history books, and biographies. Books opened a world of wonder to me at a young age, and I was fascinated by the information I could acquire. For a long time, I aspired to be a paleontologist or anthropologist. I was fascinated by lost histories and wanted to uncover them. I loved musicals, dance, and drawing. Ultimately, all of these experiences shaped me as a writer and storyteller. I grew up in a family that discussed history, music, and social justice all the time. I grew up as a critical thinker, and this combination of experiences helped develop my Afrofuturism leanings. I am a big *Matrix* and *Star Wars* fan. I liked the film *Interstellar* too. I was a big fan of the TV show *Extant* starring Halle Berry. As for books, I like Rasheedah Phillips's *Black Quantum Futurism*.

D.L.: As for recent stuff, I showed the film *Moon* by Duncan Jones to my class at Stateville. It is a great science fiction film. I love *Children of Men*. In addition, my jam is *Attack the Block*. If you have not seen that . . . definitely, track it down. If that film had come out when I was a teenager, I would have freaked out over it. I freak out about it now anyway. Comics were a huge influence. They fueled my imagination. I want to be a comic book artist forever. I discovered the X-Men in 1978, when John Byrne and Chris Claremont started their run of consecutive issues until around the mid-1980s. I stopped buying comics regularly shortly after that run was over. I always liked TV, and I have retained much information about television, film, and culture as a result. I probably watch too much TV. Shows like *Twilight Zone, Ultraman,* and *Star Trek* were my jams. As my love for comics began to wane, my love of music rose. I grew up in the 1970s and 1980s, and in the 1970s everyone listened to music all the time. My family had a huge credenza, which housed the stereo and the records. My family listened to a huge variety of music from musicals (*West Side Story* and *Jesus Christ Superstar*), to Earth Wind and Fire, to Helen Reddy. People always had stacks of 45s to play at parties. I had a couple 45s but was too young to buy a full-length album until the 1980s. I was introduced to punk and hardcore, which I fell in love with right after rap started in the mainstream. I met rap at "Rapper's Delight" by the Sugarhill Gang. I became an avid music listener and devourer. I started a band in ninth grade and have been in bands ever since. All of these elements were the building blocks of my creative spirit. I still think critically about all of the aforementioned genres. They reverberate daily. The first things I ever drew with zeal and compulsion were superheroes. Soul and funk are my heart, the way black people use to communicate their feelings across the country and communities to send messages of hope and frustrations. Punk and rap helped make me feel like a real-life superhero. Science fiction on TV helped me ask questions and let me know not having the answers was okay. The criticism that people level at musicals was the very entity that made me love the genre. My life ever since has been walking around and singing all the time.

D.D.A.: My favorite stories as a very young child were Dr. Seuss's *The Lorax*— which I have spoken about extensively as a foundation for my environmental consciousness and have used as a source in my artwork—and stories about witches, whom I loved for their quirky outsiderness. We also attended local Tiv (my ethnic group on father's side) festivals, which displayed skills in visual arts, dance, music, and costume. I bring all of this and so much more into my practice as a performance and installation artist, professor, and Afrofuturist. Right now, I am very excited about Florence Okoye (@Afrofutures_UK), who is curating and writing a series on Afrofuturism for the online magazine *How Do We Get to Next.* I am also excited about the Octavia Butler Legacy Network and the Afrofuturism Affair out of Philadelphia as well as Anais

Duplan's Center for Afrofuturist Studies, which is offering a series of residencies this year. There are so many amazing artists and exhibitions, it is impossible to keep track! This is part of the joy of Afrofuturism and the vitality that is essential to creating new futures, not only globally but also locally in Chicago.

What are your feelings on the term "Chiraq"?

D.D.A.: In terms of "Chiraq," there are many who need support and protection. The recent film is very problematic, as are some of Spike Lee's comments about what women in the present day should do in connection with the story of *Lysistrata*. For instance, the answer to the epidemic of rape on college campuses is not for women to start denying men sex. Rape is a weapon, a weapon of war; it is neither an act of intimacy nor something that women are causing. I understand the story of *Lysistrata*, and I remember how Sam Greenlee, the late author of the famous, censored *Spook Who Sat by the Door*, was working on a screenplay about *Lysistrata*. He always schooled the importance of reading Greek mythology. Spike Lee has never answered my inquiries about where he got his idea for the film, though it is quite the coincidence that it came out right after Sam's passing. I feel very protective of him, as he was a dear friend and supporter of my Black Arts Movement classes and students, and he was an example of an artist who spoke up and was ostracized and censored. We have to look at where power lies, who is telling the stories, who has access to funding and support, and which artists toil throughout their lives in obscurity and poverty. This is real life. Chicago is a war zone. We know this. I think about how Afrofuturism can be used as a pathway, and I feel now, after all these years of teaching, that I see the classroom as the Mothership, the site to dock ships and travel into other galaxies via art and from which new generations come into awareness of their history and their power to shape the future.

Note

1. Mark A. Rockeymoore, "What Is Afrofuturism?" *AuthorsDen*, February 2000, http://www.authorsden.com/visit/viewArticle.asp?id=4308.

Matthew Wilbourn

Captives public showing

Rahm I just wanna know If I'm the future
why am I so underfunded Why is it the further
from the city's loop a school. The more hoops
they jump through to keep the lights on. Hoped
to keep teachers in the game. When you taking
them out Some left to bleachers of the suburbs
Where it safe No false preachers with false promise
Promise annual pay raise But couldn't deliver Cash
cow Chicago has more beef than Drake and meek mill
But we just get the liver To cps I'm worth 73 cents
on every dollar a suburban kid gets That three fifths
equates to three-fifths of a human But I am whole
I am not three-fifths or half Put my mom under contract
And cut pay That's food off my table I don't care
if I'm labeled another mad black kid in the city
with no resources Sorry But your forced starvation
has made me hungry for the food on your table
Made me resourceful And that byrd Bennett take
Nothing else from my nest Because if she really black
she know we spray raid on pests And she bugging
me Head of cps but kids go private not like her actions
We can't be proactive to something we can't see
She washed her hands of us Yet we still can't get soap
in our bathrooms a pontius pilate of perplexing portions
She didn't want to deal with us anyway Cps
Why hold employees to standards you can't meet
Sets schools up for failure with demands they cannot meet
And these are in places where drugs is the one thing
that guarantees ends meet But I'm no expert

I ride the green line through the meat packing district
Headed to Harlem on Lake Street I see Empty lots
til Garfield park Then more empty plots In those I see

what shoulda coulda would've been In a city of big shoulders
I see not one pair trying to fix it Yea we have Barber conversations
Then we cut and dismiss it We had a shot but most just watched
it come and missed it Cps Children put to slaughter
Criminal pipeline systems Corruption polluted schools
Corrupt people sanctioned over us With none of our experience

I dared Rahm to make an experiment with his kids
Bring them to the hood We'll roll out the red carpet
Give them Timberlands for the snow Robins rocks
and trues too It only matters Give them only our finest
Only our finest food Pizza puffs Uncle Remus
Harold chicken and See thru kitchen Bet they won't
make it Bet they can't take it Too pampered to feel
the struggle of being hampered by unseen forces
and diet ripping your insides and arteries

But this all isn't hard for me
                              Cps
Why make the road to success
so far for me

THE FUTURE OF CHICAGO

Idris Goodwin

Ghost Town

The ancestors still here
They with us

All eras' greats and grands
Their voices gagged

Lynched
Squeezed
Caught between crosshairs
Or poison
Or strays

All eras' silent and unremarkable
Unfulfilled and intimidated

Centuries of them
Their untold stories
Unactualized visions

The city got ghosts

They don't interfere just watch
Watch and move through us
Though when we quiet enough we can hear them

Inhabiting the emptied
factories and public high schools
That once bustled with promise of prosperity

They watch
how we scheme and holler at our frequent haunts

They see
how we bullshit and medicate and try to keep the fire alive

They know
what secrets been filed away
what confessions suppressed
and witnesses made to look away

But we
Can't hide shit from those who travel in the particles
Who dance and drift among this city of the forgetful

But when we sleep they invade our dreams
Our dreams are the ghosts begging to be resurrected

They whisper gets caught in our heart
When open wide enough

They'll guide our hands toward discovery
our voices toward unisons of dissent
harmonies of evolution

Through us they resurrect

They'll never again fill in fabrics
and pull oxygen

Through us they'll see their dreams material
Through us they'll see heaven

Through them we learn our names
Through them we learn honor
Through them we learn mistakes
Through them we learn how to fight

Through them we'll make heaven
Through them we'll resurrect

Sarah McKee

Mama Emily tells the story

Emily Lansana is a longtime member of the Chicago community, originally hailing from Cleveland, Ohio. Her life has been concentrated around the arts, leading her to become both a professional storyteller with the National Association of Black Storytellers and Associate Director of Community Arts Engagement for the David Logan Center for the Arts. The artistic legacy does not stop here: her sons are active members in Louder Than a Bomb (whose team she has coached to finals twice) and Young Chicago Authors. I have recently become friends with one of her sons, and he gave me the opportunity to ask her a series of questions through email about her life, her work, and her city.

Have you always been interested in the arts? Why did you decide to make storytelling your primary focus?

I came from a family that supported music. I played many different instruments, but music was not my gift. I started performing poetry and theater at a young age. I went into storytelling because I felt that as an actor, I did not have the kind of ownership that I wanted to have over the art I created and way that I performed it. I enjoy the way that I am able to shape and share stories.

Who have been some of your major influences and why?

My parents, who valued education, influenced me. I was blessed to have committed public school teachers who nurtured my creativity. I was impacted by a theater teacher at Karamu, the black theater company, and by my mentor at the program at Northwestern University, who taught me that success in the arts is connected to discipline and hard work. I have also been impacted by an appreciation for creating community, valuing young people, and recognizing that the arts can be powerful. At Yale, I had the opportunity to connect with significant African American scholars and a supportive community of African American students, which helped me to develop my political consciousness.

When did you move to Chicago? What are some of the primary differences and similarities between Chicago and Cleveland?

I moved to Chicago after I graduated from Yale. Chicago is a much more diverse community than Cleveland—culturally, economically, and in opportunity. Chicago is a very complicated city in terms of its neighborhoods. The area that we first lived in on the South Side is near 79th and Cottage Grove, which is a community that my aunt and uncle moved into many, many years ago. They were the first African Americans to move onto the block. Today, Chicago is a community that struggles with violence and poverty; however, there are many committed people who are working to address these issues. The neighborhood we lived in on the West Side was a diverse working-class neighborhood, with people of all different cultures. It is rare to find that kind of community in Chicago, where things tend to be segregated.

How do you think Chicago differs from the time and place your sons are growing up in now to when you first moved here?

I moved to Chicago in 1988, straight out of college. I think that in many ways, the city is very different, but many things are the same. There are still huge differences between the Haves and Have Nots. There is still a great deal of segregation. I believe there are cultural opportunities and more places for young people to express themselves. There are programs like Gallery 37, After School Matters, and Young Chicago Authors. Places like Millennium Park and the MCA have all developed during the time that I have lived in Chicago, so I have been able to see some exciting transformations. Chicago is home to some major African American cultural institutions that have influenced me and continue to thrive: these are places like ETA Creative Arts Foundation Third World Press, the DuSable Museum, and newer institutions like Congo Square Theatre.

But raising four black boys in Chicago means that I think about violence every day. I've thought about it since before they were born. I thought about it when they were babies and worried about them hearing gunshots. I thought about it when they were little ones in terms of when and where they could play. I think about it in terms of where and when it is safe for them to move through the city alone. I think about it in terms of where we live. However, I also believe that there are many wonderful things about Chicago, which is why I choose to stay here. I do not honestly believe that Chicago is significantly different from most places in this country. Trayvon Martin was killed in a gated community. Tamir Rice was killed on a seemingly quiet playground. America is a challenging place for all people of color.

What do you want your children to see in the future of Chicago—a post-"Chiraq" era? What do you see for the future of Chicago?

I love the fact that there are so many brilliant young people making things happen in the city. I want my sons to believe that it is possible for them to realize their dreams and to be influenced by a community that supports their growth. I hope that we will learn to value life, recognize, and honor our differences in deeper and more meaningful ways. I think that the arts play a critical role in human development and survival; I hope that we will continue to support arts education and artistic expression.

Grace Jones

Out the Trap
Building with the Elephant Rebellion

The Elephant Rebellion is a collective of artists & activists dedicated to empowering communities through arts and education. A multiethnic crew in the Upton neighborhood, one of the most and only racially and socioeconomically diverse neighborhoods in Chicago, the Elephant Rebellion began organizing in 2012 after the tragic death of rapper-poet and former Louder Than a Bomb champion John Vietnam Nguyen.

Some say "Chiraq" is a misnomer or the media's attempt to blow out of proportion and generalize the dangers of the streets. Others claim it describes their life to a T: they are living in a war zone. To a Chicagoan, the word need not be explained or defined. Whether or not one agrees with the term, the experience that lies behind it is a familiar one for many living in the city. In a discussion with Uptown hip-hop and community youth empowerment group Elephant Rebellion, members share their thoughts and experiences.

Cinematographer and photographer Charles J. Williams grew up in the Robert Taylor Homes. When the public housing units were shut down to eventually be replaced by million-dollar single homes, Charles and his family moved to the outskirts of Chicago along with many Southsiders being edged out. Charles dubs the experience that followed "hood suburban life."

"Gentrification is a double-edged sword," he says. The statement is echoed by a series of drawn-out *truuuue* responses from the others in the room. Charles admits that the Bronzeville neighborhood of the projects was not a safe one, nor were the conditions up to par. The inhabitants, however, were severely penalized by attempts to "clean up" parts of the city. "They moved out everybody. But it was only a small few that were bad. The projects were messed up. But those were young folk. A lot of the South Side was forty-year-olds, grandmothers who kept to themselves and were family oriented and neighborhood oriented. Some youth made it worse than it is and that gets magnified."

Mawael "Mo" Michaels, now a music producer and Elephant Rebellion's Director of Music Development, moved from East Africa to Chicago at a young age. He says that the North Side and the South Side are not in competition for death tolls or for which part of the city is "most dangerous." "Just being Black, just wearing the color blue was a nightmare because that was the opposite gang color," Mo says, reflecting on his childhood in West Rogers Park. "Coming from school, coming from Walgreens, because the uniform I had to wear was a blue and black outfit, the train rides were very intimidating at times because I would have people thinking I was representing colors. I may not have been getting robbed, attacked, or jumped even though it's come close. I may have just been lucky, but I had to deal with just some awkward moments because of those things. And I think that's just Chicago in general."

Mo is quiet for a few moments, then hands the recorder over to a fellow Elephant to fill the silence. Before he gives it up to them entirely, he pulls the microphone back to his lips for one definitive afterthought. "It should not be called Chiraq," he whispers.

Uran Kabashi, a rapper and treasurer for Elephant Rebellion, receives the recorder and gives his take on growing up in Chicago. Kabashi immigrated from Kosovo to Chicago's North Side in 1999. "On the topic of gangs, when I first got here, my cousin and Mo's cousin were heavily into that shit so I was introduced to gang life, smoking weed, and all that. Two of my cousins were gangbanging and incidentally got introduced to Mo's cousins. He and I were the little kids like, 'Look, this is our role models!' [My cousins] are good people, they just enjoyed that life. I don't know why they didn't find a home at home, because they had something to have them find a family. They had the family support, and in some ways the family showed them care, but—"

"They wanted to live a certain lifestyle," Mo chimes in. "That means you have to leave the home, which is why I hate the word 'Chiraq' sometimes. It makes regular people not realize what good they have at home, and they want to participate in a certain lifestyle that's portrayed in media, and it makes it cool. With my cousin at least, hip-hop, hop boys, the trap side of hip-hop really made them think that was how you had to be cool and represented."

"It's finding self-esteem in self-destructive ways," says Kabashi. The conversation turns to the artistic culture that has grown around the street life, both condemned and revered by many. "Drill music represents the lifestyle for sure," says Kabashi.

Charles leans into the microphone. "On the subject of music, you know what term I really hate? I really hate, and I feel like we've kind of accepted but—"

"Trap?"

"Yes."

"It is what it is, though," says Mo matter-of-factly. "It's like somebody is telling you a message like 'Yo, I'm struggling,' but then somebody else turns that message around and glamorizes it."

The term "trap" refers to a place where drugs are created and served. The downward spiral in life caused by these "traps" is almost impossible to escape, notoriously so.

"I hate it because it is what it is. Once you get in it, you get hooked, you're not coming back," says Charles gravely. "Well, you can, it's hard; it's a trap. So understanding what 'the trap' is and then relating that to music and the lifestyle and people using it as pop culture is kind of fucked up to me."

"We can talk about the devil, but we're not worshipping the devil," counters ER rapper Jarvis. Although he agrees that "trap" has come to represent a detrimental lifestyle, he fails to peg it as entirely negative.

"The gang life at first, it was something that was positive. You're protecting your community because when the slaves were first released, it was really segregated. You have Italians that were coming—they were trying to make a name for themselves—you have that community right next to a Black community right next to a Jewish community.

"The gang mentality was 'We want to protect our community if someone's gonna mess with us.' And obviously it got corrupted, and it is what it is now. Now it's become this thing where you're forced into it and you're in it because they get you like, 'You want to be part of this brotherhood, right? It's nothing bad, you know. . . .' It's a good way to get quick money if your parents are struggling, you don't want to see that. They're not selling drugs because they want to, they're selling drugs because their parents need to keep the lights on."

Dealing becomes a network through which people depend on one another for business. "Let's say you get into it, you the man with the drugs and you hit your goal. Let's say you have a million dollars and you want to get out. But people are depending on you to make their money and now you tryna get out and you can't."

Charles dubs this the "crabs in a barrel" phenomenon.

In most conversations about Chiraq, a paradox arises between the realism of the term and the perception of the problem. Although many living in the heart of violence long for their voices to be heard and their struggle to be acknowledged, the attention that Chiraq has garnered is not positive. Instead of shedding light on a dark truth, it has put many of the contributors in the spotlight of celebrity. It has created a stigma that overshadows many of Chicago's attributes.

"Chicago is the most segregated city in the U.S.," points out Kabashi.

"If you look at the layout you see why," responds Charles. "Geographically. North vs. South. We have to have these symbols. So Chicago becomes Chi-raq. It becomes this problem that is very systematic, but we like to point out certain problems because we don't actually have to deal with the problem so we can say, 'Chicago is the problem.' We don't look at the problems, we put it on the symbols."

They believe that the media is the main perpetrator of misconceptions about Chicago. Amplified through the lens of the camera, important issues are turned to fuel for speculation. Mo's sister lives in China, and her consumption of Chicago-centered news leads her to worry for her brother.

"She's always telling me to cut my dreads off because she's like 'I know what's happening in Chicago, there's all these gang violences, you're gonna go hang out with your friends one day and they're gonna mistake you and you're gonna get shot.' And I seriously see that sort of stuff, that concern coming from her watching CNN, her watching local news and there's this trend. It's a trend. Hashtag trend. Even people who don't know in detail, they'll be like 'Yeah! Chicago is bad!' They don't know details or anything. It's this thing that the media is really focusing on, it pushes it pushes it pushes. . . ."

When asked to predict Chicago's future in one sentence, each artist exceeds the limit.

"I see Chicago as the center of so many things. In Chicago I see different cultures, different types of people in it. To me it's gonna become a true representation of what actually America is. It's a diverse city, and I don't see that a lot of places. But it's also segregated," says Mo.

"We're gonna empower ourselves and our community through the power of arts and education. Because the artists are very conscious," states Kabashi.

Sabrina, another member of Elephant Rebellion, joins the conversation. "From an outside perspective, coming from New York, seeing what the education system is like in New York City, there's a vast difference. Over here it kinda sucks. I see Chicago as a city of progress because there's so much progress than can still be made that other states have made, and this city is such a big city. And it's known as the Second City but it kinda gets pushed to the side and not noticed so much. That's the reason why there's so much progress to be made."

"I see it as a city of progress. I see it as a city that can teach a message to people because they have this image of Chicago, and we all here in this room know that it's not true, in our city we know that it's not true. There are no parts of my city that I don't feel comfortable walking down. Even the worst parts of my city I don't feel uncomfortable walking there. If we can get the message out that it's not that way and really show a true representation of what the city is, then we can highlight this bigger problem of us rushing to judgment and believing what the media puts in front of us, and think for ourselves," concludes Jarvis.

Rapper Citizen X adds his perspective: "Based off everything I've seen recently in my city as far as everyone coming together and speaking as a whole, I would say the future of this city is bright. I would say as long as we continue to fight for what we need as a community, as a city, I don't see any reason, I don't see any reason Chicago couldn't become the number one city in the United States."

Jahnari Pruitt

Paradise on fire

No I don't think heaven would be a paradise Not in the way they told us Not a floating cloud with your name on it and a God that loved you enough to let you in his church

No I don't think it would be a paradise Not something to write an ode for In fact It wouldn't be anything at all And there wouldn't be bodies Nor would there be bibles What use would we have for such things There would just be memories Playing over And over And over Like burning film reels Or fireflies too close to campfires one summer in '07

I think it would just be a space big enough to spark in In fact everything would just be burning sacred and combusting In fact everything would just be the sun

And each person would just be a flare that could dance its own dance and be as brilliant as it wanted to be And hopefully it could burn an afterimage on someone's memory And there would be no nightclub to turn to ashes and tears in Or a driver's seat to slowly become carbon dioxide and nitrogen in

It would not be a paradise. But at least there would be room to burn To call all ye faithful to the combustion To wash feet in the smoke To be made New as Joan of Arc Remember how she prayed on the pyre How she screamed "Jesus Jesus Jesus" And no one No one at all came to her But Here Here we would need no one to come for us Here we would have no use for a savior Not in nowhere Where sin wouldn't exist Where we would only have the memories that everyone else in the world forgot Where we would craft a church from the ember Where there would be no body to be shackled to Just a soul to revel in No It would not be a paradise.

But it would be bright Like funeral pyre bright Like flames so bright that it blinds and sears all the sin off Fire so hot that you don't even feel the flames as they lick you holy again

Like fire so hot they turn blue and blue is the color of healing so you know that it's right And beautiful And truer than that other place you came from so it's okay to stay Here and glimmer and be a lightning bug above a camp-fire slowly becoming holy again.

Yana Kunichoff and Sarah Macaraeg

How to Win Reparations

Chicago's Model Legislation and Where Activists Have Their Sights Set Next

Somewhere between his twelfth and thirteenth hour inside a Chicago Police interrogation room, Lindsey Smith decided to confess to a murder he didn't commit. The year was 1972. Multiple officers had pistol-whipped, stomped on, and beaten him again and again. Convinced he would not otherwise live to see sunlight, Smith signed a false confession for the attempted murder of a twelve-year-old white boy. At seventeen, Smith, too, was a boy. But with one major difference: he was Black.

Tried as an adult and convicted, Smith took a plea deal and served nearly five years in prison.

He was among the first of at least 120 young, primarily Black men whom Chicago police officers would torture into false confessions. Yet while many who suffer at the hands of the police never get justice, Smith's story ended differently. More than forty years later, following the passage of historic reparations legislation, he became one of the first Black people in the United States to be granted reparations for racial violence.

After receiving parole, Smith moved out of the city and attempted to rebuild his life. But his struggles were far from over. Given the conviction on his record, Smith faced difficulty in everything from finding work to accessing car insurance benefits. And he remained haunted by his experiences as a teen inside the interrogation room and never felt at ease in Chicago again—until May 7, 2015.

On that date, the City of Chicago signed into law an ordinance granting cash payments, free college education, and a range of social services to fifty-seven living survivors of police torture. Explicitly defined as reparations, the ordinance also includes a mandate to teach the broader public about the torture, through a memorial and public schools curriculum, and a formal apology from Mayor Rahm Emanuel. The hard-won legislation, envisioned by activists, made Chicago the first and thus far only municipality in the country to pay reparations for racist police violence.

"I can sleep a whole lot better tonight," Smith told local media upon the bill's passage.[1] A sixty-one-year-old factory worker, he has since collected $100,000 in reparations.

"I'd take that night back before I took their money any day. I can never get back that time away from my family and the things I could have done," Smith said. "But at least I can afford new shoes now."

As the national conversation around racial disparities in the United States has broadened to include criminalization, job discrimination, school segregation, and neglect of infrastructure, so has the need for a reckoning with the institutional wrongs done to African American communities. Reparations, the concept of offering monetary or social redress for historical injustices, has found a renewed life in American public discourse, and at the heart of some social movements.

With the election of Donald Trump, it seems unlikely that reparations will move forward at the national scale any time soon. But Chicago's ordinance provides a model for creating reparations on the local level, even in the face of daunting obstacles.

The momentum has been building for years. Reparations sparked debate on the presidential campaign trail, and when more than fifty organizations collaborated to write the Movement for Black Lives policy platform in 2016, they put reparations front and center.

"We wanted to put forth a set of policies that show what we really want and what would lead to a transformation of our conditions," says Karl Kumodzi, a member of the coalition's policy table who is active with the organizations BlackBird and BYP100 in Brooklyn, New York. "Reparations had to be at the forefront of that."

Since then, a Georgetown University committee has recognized that the school profited from the sale of slaves and said it would "reconcile" by naming two buildings after African Americans and by offering preferred admission status to any descendants of slaves who worked at the university. Whether or not Georgetown's plans offer true recompense is in contention. "You don't admit you owe someone money and repay them with lottery tickets," wrote sociologist Tressie McMillan Cottom.[2]

Increasingly, the question appears not to be whether reparations are needed, but in what form and how to get them.

Most of the time, it's still an abstract conversation. But Chicago's $5.5 million reparations legislation is a concrete exception.

According to a city spokesperson, as of October 2016 payments have been made to the majority of the fifty-seven recognized survivors, nine individuals have begun the process of potentially accessing free community college, and eleven requests for prioritized access to social services have been made. Meanwhile, a city-funded community center dedicated to survivors and their families opened in 2017, and curriculum on the torture scandal is being taught in Chicago Public Schools.

From the Black Manifesto to the Movement for Black Lives

Mary Frances Berry, a former chairperson of the U.S. Civil Rights Commission, documented the country's first struggle for reparations, which was led by ex-slaves, in her book *My Face Is Black Is True*.[3] She thinks Chicago offers a model for how to win reparations across the country.

"We often hear talk about national legislation and national responses in the civil rights community. . . . But a lot of things can be done locally," she says. "Chicago shows [what] can be done—and [that] other kinds of remedies for other kinds of harms can be done, like for example the harm done to the people in Flint." Berry was referencing the ongoing water crisis in Flint, Michigan, that left thousands of residents in the predominantly African American town without access to clean drinking water.

Not far from Flint, nearly fifty years ago, the Black Manifesto launched in Detroit as one of the first calls for reparations in the modern era, penned by James Forman, a former organizer with the Student Nonviolent Coordinating Committee, a key Civil Rights group.[4] Released at the 1969 Black Economic Development Conference, the manifesto demanded $500 million in reparations from predominantly white religious institutions for their historic role in perpetuating slavery. The manifesto asserted that the money would fund nine key projects, aimed at building the collective wealth of Black communities: a Black university, Black presses and broadcast networks, research and training centers, and a southern land bank. A multiracial contingent of clergy in support of the Black Manifesto succeeded in raising at least $215,000 from the Episcopalian and Methodist churches, through months of rancorous deliberation—that ultimately tore the coalition apart.

The mantle was next assumed by the National Coalition of Blacks for Reparations in America, or N'COBRA. Centering their demands on reparations for chattel slavery, N'COBRA gained a hearing throughout the early 1990s, but their demands never garnered a mainstream foothold.

Joe Feagin, distinguished professor of sociology at Texas A&M University, has a hunch about why that is. It has been difficult for demands for reparations for slavery to gain traction in the past, he says, because the direct link between slavery and the high rates of poverty prevalent in contemporary Black communities is not widely understood, let alone acknowledged.

"When you focus on slavery, it's easy for whites to say all the whites are dead and all the Blacks are dead," Feagin said. In other words, it's easy to dismiss the idea as water under the bridge.

"That is not true for Jim Crow segregation," Feagin said, citing a study on "segregation stress syndrome" based on interviews with 100 elderly African

Americans in the South.[5] The study revealed that 80 percent of the participants' families had suffered extreme violence in the form of lynching, rape, attempted rape, and home invasions. "They can name the white families who were involved," Feagin said. "Without knowing the whole story you can't know that whites are unjustly enriched, blacks unjustly impoverished—and that that has to be repaired," Feagin said. "What allows us whites to get off the hook is nobody knows this history, so we can make absurd statements like 'slavery happened hundreds of years ago,'" Feagin said of arguments against reparations.

But with the publication in 2014 of Ta-Nehisi Coates's landmark article "The Case for Reparations," the living legacy of white supremacy became difficult to deny.[6] Detailing the systematic "plunder" of Black communities, Coates's work tracks multiple Chicagoans living the outcomes of generations of racism—demonstrating a legacy of impoverishment that runs from slavery, sharecropping, and Jim Crow to housing discrimination and economic hardship today.

As for solutions, Coates called for support of H.R.40, federal legislation that sought to form a commission on reparations. Sponsored by Democrat John Conyers of Michigan, ranking member of the House Judiciary Committee and a founding member of the Congressional Black Caucus, H.R.40 aimed "to examine the institution of slavery and its legacy, like racial disparities in education, housing, and healthcare" and then "recommend appropriate remedies to Congress." First introduced in 1989, H.R.40 has been reintroduced by Conyers in every session of Congress since—and subsequently has been mired in the House's Subcommittee on the Constitution and Civil Justice, currently chaired by Republican Trent Franks of Arizona.[7]

But although H.R.40 has languished, other reparations legislation has prevailed at both the state and federal levels. In 1988, President Ronald Reagan signed a bill providing $20,000 to each of the approximately 65,000 living Japanese Americans who had been interned during World War II, prompting Congress to allocate $1.25 billion. A few years later, the state of Florida approved $2.1 million dollars for the living survivors of a 1923 racial pogrom that resulted in multiple deaths and the complete decimation of the Black community in the town of Rosewood. More recently, in 2014, the state of North Carolina set aside $10 million for reparations payments to living survivors of the state's eugenics program, which forcibly sterilized approximately 7,600 people. The practice was widely adopted across thirty-three states, sterilizing an estimated 60,000 people without their consent. Last year, the state of Virginia followed North Carolina's lead and will soon begin awarding $25,000 to each survivor.

Meanwhile, the five-point outline for reparations in the Movement for Black Lives platform broadens the conversation. From a demand for services focused on healing from trauma to access to free education and cash support in the form of a "guaranteed livable income," the policy platform was built on decades of experience, research, and values long held by the Black radical tradition—galvanized further by the victory in Chicago, says Karl Kumodzi.

"I got chills," he says about the day he heard the Chicago ordinance was signed. "What they won offers clear examples of reparations being more than just a check, but rather a set of initiatives and investments that address the economic, psychological, educational, and health impacts of the harm that's been done," Kumodzi says.

How They Did It

So how'd they do it?

According to sociologist Tressie McMillan Cottom, there are three key components to a reparations program: acknowledgment, restitution, and closure. In addition, for an offered recompense to be reparations, it must be specific to alleviating or directing resources at the harm caused.[8]

In many ways, the movement for reparations in Chicago started out of a lack of recognition. Communities in Chicago had spent years fighting for legal redress for survivors of police torture under Commander Jon Burge and his officers, who for nearly three decades tortured more than 100 black and Latino men into confessing to crimes they didn't commit.

Their first effort was legal—to get Burge into a courtroom despite the fact that the statute of limitations had expired on many of the alleged cases of police torture, and to achieve retrials where possible for the wrongfully convicted people still imprisoned.

The second was to make sure the torture would never be forgotten. Attorney Joey Mogul had been litigating Burge cases for more than two decades by the time the commander was finally brought into court.

But looking around at the torture survivors she had been working with, especially those asked to dredge up painful memories for the trial, she realized the victory of his conviction for perjury and obstruction of justice was a hollow one.

"It didn't bring them peace or relief," said Mogul. She points to the case of Anthony Holmes, who was tortured by officers under Burge in 1973 and went on to serve the full thirty-year sentence before being exonerated. "Anthony Holmes . . . struggles with trauma to this day. There are no psychological services for him whatsoever."

The first steps toward the ordinance began not explicitly geared toward getting reparations in Chicago but rather to collect ideas for how to memorialize the cases and make sure that Chicagoans knew of the history of police torture that scarred African American and Latino communities in the city. Mogul and a handful of torture survivors and other people who had been involved in the movement to bring Burge to justice started the Chicago Torture Justice Memorials (CTJM) as a vehicle to start collecting ideas.

From there, the idea took shape of drafting a city ordinance as a way to recognize the harm done—and bringing in reparations as the answer began to form. "I feel like reparations is a really simple concept," said Alice Kim, an academic and activist whose longtime work organizing with Burge survivors was pivotal in the CTJM and eventually the reparations ordinance. "It's repairing harm that was done."

The first draft of the ordinance was sketched out in 2012, with the explicit aim of calling for reparations—inspired by Mogul's colleague, lawyer Stan Willis, who had been active with N'COBRA and first raised the demand.

The reparations package aimed to fill in the gaps where legal efforts had fallen short. It included key practical requests like financial compensation but also a curriculum that would teach about the Burge tortures in Chicago Public Schools and free enrollment in the city's public college program.

The ordinance, in the spirit of the longtime organizing efforts, laid the bulk of responsibility at the city's feet. "The chain of command in City Hall never stopped to investigate and redress the torture," said Mogul.

It's fitting, then, that what helped spur activists to introduce the ordinance was the mayor's attempt to close the book on police torture. In October 2013, the city's finance committee had just settled a $12.3 million suit with police torture victims Ronald Kitchens and Marvin Reeves.[9] A journalist with the *Chicago Sun-Times* asked Mayor Rahm Emanuel if the police torture deserved an apology. In response Emanuel apologized—before he deflected, saying, "Let us all now move on."[10] The comment outraged activists who had been devising a proposal for justice. "We can't move on, there has been nothing done to meet the material needs of torture survivors," Mogul recalled thinking.

The group found a City Council member friendly with the mayor—Alderman Joe Moreno—to introduce the ordinance in October 2013. The ordinance would then be stuck in committee until a burst of growth in the movement pushed it out.

A coalition began taking shape in early 2014—Amnesty International brought its national platform to the project that April. By the end of 2015, a local coalition called We Charge Genocide would bring the burgeoning power of the Black Lives Matter movement to the fight for reparations. Janae

Bonsu, a member of Black Youth Project 100, organized with the fight for reparations. "If anyone is deserving of reparations, it's them," said Bonsu of the families receiving a portion of recompense.

The group upped their efforts, holding a bitterly cold Valentine's Day rally in 2015 and beseeching Emanuel, whose political future looked increasingly uncertain as he was heading into a mayoral run-off, to "have a heart."

Within a month of that February rally, the coalition met with the city three times to negotiate on the reparations package while continuing to hold public protests. A key demand was a hearing on the ordinance. "We wanted the public to have their say. We got a hearing date for April 14th," said Mogul, but "on the eve of the hearing we ultimately reached and agreed on a reparations package."

The package eventually passed, offering cash payments, a formal apology, promise to teach the history of police torture in Chicago Public Schools, and funds for the creation of the community counseling center for survivors opening on the city's South Side in 2017.

"No one believed it would pass, no one thought Emanuel would be OK with it and succumb to the pressure he ended up succumbing to. But you move your target and your people from what everybody expects, and you make the improbable possible," said Mariame Kaba, whose connection to both long-term Burge organizing efforts and the Black Lives Matter movement made her a key figure in the upswell of actions leading to the passage of the ordinance in 2015.

"We fought outside the legal box," said Mogul. "What we gained, what we won, was more expansive than any court could have provided."

On January 4, 2016, the checks to individual torture victims went into the mail. A young social worker, Camesha Jones, was hired to lead a needs assessment among survivors and their families to figure out how the forthcoming community center could best meet the needs of those affected by police torture. The city agreed to provide three additional years of funding and, in the meantime, planning for the curriculum and public memorial commenced,

However, the ordinance limits financial relief to those people tortured during Burge's exact years on the force—between May 1, 1972, and November 30, 1991—despite evidence that it continued under his former subordinates. And more than twenty known Burge survivors remain incarcerated today, according to lawyers with the reparations committee.

For the CTJM team the gains of reparations serve as a starting point and reminder of all there is to be done.

"The glass is only half full because until we get those other brothers back to court and get fair and impartial hearings into their allegations of having been tortured," said Darryl Cannon, a survivor of Burge's police torture, "then this fight must continue."

The future of the reparations campaign looks both like a push for continuing education and activism. Mogul and Alice Kim are writing a book about the organizing that led to the ordinance.[11] Mogul says it's important that they opened the door, but that "others should open it further."

Moving Forward

Aislinn Pulley, a cofounder of Black Lives Matter Chicago, considers the city's effort one of the most powerful examples of reparations. "Chicago . . . created new possibilities of what transformative justice, holistic justice can look like and in addressing the modern problems of policing, helps us envision new demands and possibilities of justice," she said.

What's more, activists like Janae Bonsu, who worked on the reparations campaign, have taken their experience in Chicago and run with it. As a member of the 100 Black Youth Project, she has fought in recent months to keep open the historically black Chicago State University in Illinois and to partially "defund the police" in municipal budgets nationwide, advocating for the funding of programs benefitting Black communities in need of services instead.

Bonsu sees clear next steps for where the fight for reparations needs to move, saying, "I think the conversation [on] reparations should be expanded to thinking about the War on Drugs, in thinking about [housing] redline policies—in all the ways systemic racism can be proved."

The story of Chicago's ordinance suggests that local campaigns have the potential to broaden reparations in each of these ways. But in the absence of a national policy, how much harm can be mitigated by local laws? If hundreds of Chicago-style ordinances were replicated in every town or state where demonstrable systemic harm can be proved, how far would they go in addressing centuries of wrong meted out by the state against African Americans and other vulnerable communities?

Karl Kumodzi says that reparations are needed on multiple fronts—reparations for both specific harms, such as those wrought by Chicago's police torture ring, and oppressive systems as a whole. "What we think is really needed is an analysis of reparations, not just for very specific cases where you have to prove it," he says, but also for the intergenerational, community-wide and lasting impacts of systems like slavery and policing. "They also have the same consequences, the same needs of their families—the same lasting traumatic effects."

However, under a Trump presidency, Kumodzi says, priorities in organizing will shift because conditions have shifted. "Fights that we could take on and things that we could try to win a month ago are things that just won't happen in the next four years at the federal level," he acknowledges. But Kumodzi also sees organizing at the state and city levels as a powerful means for keeping the larger dream of national reparations alive.

"Our vision for the world that we want to live in, our demands, our understanding of the policies that are going to get us toward that vision, that's not going to change, that's gonna stay the same for the long haul—whether it's four years, two years, ten years," he said. "There's been a lot of harms. Reparations have to be done to address those harms."

A version of this article was initially published in YES! Magazine

Notes

1. "Lindsey Smith on the Jon Burge Torture Reparations—'I Can Sleep a Whole Lot Better Tonight,'" WGNRadio.com, May 7, 2015; http://wgnradio.com/2015/05/07/lindsey-smith-on-the-jon-burge-torture-reparations-i-can-sleep-a-whole-lot-better-tonight/.

2. Tressie McMillan Cottom, "Georgetown's Slavery Announcement Is Remarkable. But It's Not Reparations," Vox.com, September 2, 2016; https://www.vox.com/2016/9/2/12773110/georgetown-slavery-admission-reparations.

3. Mary Frances Berry, *My Face Is Black Is True: Callie House and the Struggle for Ex-Slave Reparations* (New York: Alfred A. Knopf, 2005).

4. Black National Economic Development Conference, "Black Manifesto," *New York Review of Books*, July 10, 1969; http://www.nybooks.com/articles/1969/07/10/black-manifesto/.

5. Ruth K. Thompson-Miller, "Jim Crow's Legacy: Segregation Stress Syndrome," Ph.D. diss., Texas A&M University, 2011; http://oaktrust.library.tamu.edu/bitstream/handle/1969.1/ETD-TAMU-2011-05-9215/THOMPSON-MILLER-DISSERTATION.pdf?sequence=2.

6. Ta-Nehisi Coates, "The Case for Reparations," *Atlantic*, June 2014; http://www.theatlantic.com/magazine/archive/2014/06/the-case-for-reparations/361631/.

7. The most recent version of the bill may be found at https://www.congress.gov/bill/115th-congress/house-bill/40.

8. Cottom, "Georgetown's Slavery Announcement."

9. People's Law Office, "Finance Committee Approves $12.3 Million Settlement With Police Torture Victims Ronald Kitchen and Marvin Reeves,"

press release; http://peopleslawoffice.com/finance-committee-approves-12
-3-million-settlement-with-police-torture-victims-ronald-kitchen-and-marvin
-reeves/.

10. Fran Spielman and Tina Sfondeles, "Emanuel Apologizes for Torture under former Chicago Police Commander, Cohorts," *Chicago Sun-Times*, September 1, 2013; reposted at http://www.nodeathpenalty.org /news-and-updates/emanuel-apologizes-torture-under-former-chicago-police -commander-cohorts.

11. See https://www.opensocietyfoundations.org/about/programs /us-programs/grantees/alice-kim-and-joey-mogul.

Jamila Woods
BY & BY

after Jeanann Verlee & Martin Espada

will the will the will the will the circle
be unbroken, by & by, by & by
there's a better better world a waitin
in the in the sky oh, in the sky

fifty mothballed buildings stand empty-bellied AND padlocks swing from
their necks AND there are gymnasiums full of cardboard boxes full of retired
globes & rulers AND they call it "phasing out" AND there is a *school desert*
in Bronzeville AND somehow Charters poke through the sand like daisies
AND the parking lots fill with recycling bins AND fifty mothballed buildings
stand empty bellied AND where will the children go? AND receiving schools
burst at the seams AND teachers teach in storage closets AND police watch
kids walk home AND they call them "welcoming schools" AND the blueprint
for Obama College Prep looks like the Bell Curve AND fifty buildings with
eyes blotted out & boarded up AND all blackboards erased AND all black
children bused across gang lines AND "get off the bus & run" AND all brown
children bused across gang lines AND "No Child Left Behind" AND the
city holds the red pen over the South Side, West Side AND some folks' kids
will never set foot in public school AND the American flag still flies outside
shuttered Trumbull Elementary AND

will the will the will the will the broken

be a circle
            better better   sky
over my world

OR the gymnasium floor creaks under sneakers, brick bellies full again OR
Fred Hampton College Prep opens in Englewood OR "Everything you can
imagine is real" OR "strong schools mean strong communities" OR black &
brown children see themselves in their textbooks, their teachers OR building

a new Chicago means building new libraries not condos, community centers not football stadiums OR "we are not toys" nine-year-old Asean Johnson says "we are not going / down without a fight" OR Pilsen parents of Whittier Elementary School stage a sit-in for a library OR "Everything you can imagine is real" OR students are told that they are loved OR students are shown that they are loved OR students are loved OR "we are not toys"
we are not broken
we are not waiting for a better world in the sky

Kara Jackson

Somewhere, Upcoming

Tomorrow, the sun and the moon will shake hands.
Here, everything circles in compromise:

a woman can share her oven with the man who put her there.
Soon, the mothers cloak their breasts in lots of nothing,

Wear them for their babies' coos, their daily milk.
Something is holy about a body that feeds another, and here

there is no carton that can fit a woman.
The next day, the sun and the moon will share

a bed. no one loves in color, but instead,
in tune. A white woman can whistle in spite —

finds her lover here. Soon, the mouth
speaks in sounds. The day after, sun

cannot speak with its fire. The gun will
make the man, and not the reverse

so if he walks, he bloodies no one.
Soon, everyone can bleed on their own.

How a woman pays the sky her dues.
I imagine there are girls who never pain

under the weight of an eager boy. Here,
the sun doesn't bother the moon it sleeps

in the womb of the Earth.

Page May and Nate Marshall
Toward the Unreasonable

Page

I met J when he was in fourth grade. He was a joyous kid with a contagious smile. After a long conversation about identity, family, and Chicago, I asked him what he thought justice was. At first, he couldn't imagine justice without involving the police. He acknowledged a need for "better cops" but still articulated justice through a dependency on police and prisons.

I decided to personalize the question for him. I asked what he would do if I stole something of his—like his favorite toy. What if he knew it was me, but I refused to admit it? I asked him what he would need to happen to feel like "justice was served."

J paused, his smile breaking for the first time. He said he wouldn't call the cops. He said he would pester me, over and over until I admitted what I'd done and apologized. He added that I'd need to replace his toy. I asked if that was enough, since the "crime" was solved and his stuff was returned. He laughed.

He said it wouldn't be enough to just have his stuff back because I'd done more than taken his toy, I'd also broken our friendship. He went on saying he'd go on vacation to turn up with his family and that while he was having a great time and enjoying himself, I'd have to stay back and watch all of his valuables for him. I'd have to do this, take care of the things he most treasured, every day. And that he'd do this over and over until he trusted me again. He said justice would be complete when he could trust me again.

Nate

When I was in eighth grade I was attacked. Two of my friends and I were waiting for the bus when we were approached by a group of six kids from high school. This crew attempted to intimidate us into giving them money. Once it was clear that we wouldn't be so easily shook, they jumped us. A few seconds into the assault two of the guys stopped and called off their friends. They recognized me from the basketball courts in our hood. They said I was cool, and the other guys relented. They did, though, try to jump my other two friends (who weren't from our hood). After about a minute of a small fight between the three of us and the six of them, a car slowed down and called out and the crew of six ran.

Later that evening my mom called the police, and they came to our house. They told us nothing could be done. Even though I knew two of the guys by face and nickname, they said basically everyone in our neighborhood, myself included, fit their description.

After they left, my mom called my oldest sister and told her what happened. She reached out to some of her friends who were high-ranking gang members in our hood and told them. They knew me as a smart, studious kid who went to magnet school and was a decent pickup basketball player. By the end of the week every member of the crew that jumped us had come to my house and rung the doorbell to offer an apology. The gang members offered me a restoration that the police were unwilling or unable to offer.

Here in Chicago, we currently spend 40 percent of the city's operating budget on police. That's $4 million a day and $1.5 billion a year. To put that in perspective, that's 300 percent more than our city spends on community services—mental health services, treatment abuse, violence prevention, youth and job training programs, affordable housing, etc., combined. That's $4 million a day invested into punishment, surveillance, and criminalization. That's $4 million a day divested from our communities and the programs we need. That's $4 million in the daily political choice to prioritize punishment over healing and prevention.

We are abolitionists. Meaning, we believe in a world that does not equate police with safety or prisons with justice. We believe in a world in which prevention, repairing the harm caused, and addressing the root causes of the conflict are more important than punishment. The concept of abolition may at first seem unreasonable: "If there are no police, how will we maintain order?!" "Who will protect us?" "What about crime?"

We both had similar reactions upon first hearing the idea. To suggest a world without police and prisons seems to challenge a core understanding of the world, our sense of "normal." It seems like an unreasonable idea.

Quite simply, though, this shit isn't working. The police and prison system is, at best, a failed experiment. It has failed to keep our people safe. It has failed to reduce crime. It has failed to prevent harm. It has failed to facilitate justice. To suggest that more of the same is our best option, after hundreds of years of a horrendous track record, is the unreasonable idea.

This isn't working. It never has and really never was supposed to. One need only study the history of police in America to understand that American policing evolved from slave patrols in the South and suppressing immigrant workers' movements in the North. This is the deception of the "It's just a few bad apples" theory: the roots are toxic. The cops that chased down Laquan and detained Sandra are a part of a larger "justice" system that has always functioned to terrorize the Black community. We see—from slave patrols, to convict leasing, to lynchings, to Jim Crow & the KKK, to Selma, to the assassination of Fred Hampton, to Stonewall, to the War on Drugs, to the murder of Rekia Boyd—one thing: the police have never kept us safe.

The police are here to manage, control, and repress people, not "crime." The overwhelming and constant presence of police terror serves to normalize it—it becomes almost mundane in its routineness. The horrific spectacle of individualized instances of police violence reveals the underlying systemic relationship between marginalized communities and the State. This is a relationship of unequal access to power and resources—a relationship where police use violence to silence, isolate, control, and repress.

There is nothing normal, inevitable, or permanent about this condition.

At base, abolition is what my mother taught me. She said that "there's no such thing as monsters." I believe she's right. No one is born evil. Crime is a consequence of social, political, and economic conditions. Quite simply, "hurt people hurt people."

If we are to address these root causes, we must shift our approach to dealing with harm away from punishment and toward questions of Who was harmed? How do we help them? And how do we make sure this never happens again? We believe that transformative processes of justice will ultimately make prisons and policing obsolete.

We must first imagine it. The poet Martín Espada says, "The abolition of slave-manacles began as a vision of hands without manacles."[1] Once imagined, it becomes an idea, which can become a possibility, which can become a reality.

Part of imagining a world without police means that we have to focus on prevention. We have to focus on what happens BEFORE harm occurs. Prefiguring the world in which we want to live to make sure that we build solid and healthy relationships is critical. Without that, we'll only be replicating the police in a different way, even if the institution is dismantled.

It is important to imagine, but we must also recognize the practices of abolition all around us, historically and currently. White kids in the suburbs with a drug problem don't go to jail. Undocumented people often have to manage conflict without calling the police, out of necessity. The history of indigenous nations across the globe offers thousands of alternatives. When you look for it, you can find examples of abolition in practice everywhere.

For a safer, more just world, we must imagine a world without police and prisons. We must recognize that police are a modern tactic of State control. We must name the daily occurrences of abolition all around us. And we must commit to the long struggle of demanding and building that world which reflects our vision for community safety.

It will take time. It will take time to get the cops out of our heads and out of our hearts. It will take time to do the work of reimagining what justice means. It will take time to build up alternative systems to keep people safe. It will take time, but more than time it will take work. It will take struggle. It will take study. It will take imagination. It will take strategy. It will take organization. It will take investment in what we believe and divestment from what we do not. It will take the discipline of hope. And it will take love.

Note

1. Martín Espada, "Imagine the Angels of Bread," *Yes! Magazine*, September 30, 1999, http://www.yesmagazine.org/issues/power-of-one/2266.

Sammy Ortega

Water Pressure

On a 90+ degree day the sun decides to tie its shoe
gangbangers out again
They pack a tool
when the sun is out they open fire
hydrants
For children to run
into streets
pushed to curve
By water pressure
XL basketball shorts
falling
Midway ass cheek
Gangway filas become sponge
The law is upset
Gangbangers open fire
Never mention the
hydrants
Never mention
The day where
Most of us are safe
From fire

Dr. Haki Madhubuti

#BlackLivesMatter and . . . the Six Unconditionals
Excerpts from *Taking Bullets*

Between hurricanes and volcanoes that encase the "Black Lives Matter" movement, nothing happens unless Black lives matter. If we do not love, care, educate, and protect ourselves, especially our children, the world for us literally stops. The next all-demanding steps are that Black families, Black institutions, Black communities, Black businesses, and Black visions matter. As we fight the exterior, the interior must be created, supported, fortified, and expanded.

Where are our great Black institutions? Where are the high-achieving schools, colleges, universities, museums, medical centers, think tanks, and centers of learning that great civilizations require? There are only a few left in our communities. All others, and I do mean all of them, are in deep, deep financial and organizational trouble bordering on severe breakdown, bankruptcy, or irrelevancy. The critical, life-giving and life-saving institutional structures that feed into and sustain a people are fast disappearing from Black communities. That which is not acknowledged nationally is that the *Negroes are back in charge,* and the black lives matter movement is today's young people's answer to the failure of current Negro leadership.

The major institutions that have survived and thrived among us are Black churches. And I categorically state without reservation that Black churches are clearly not enough. Their weakness is not found in their traditional mission of providing spiritual guidance, bonding traditions, family rituals, psychological support, and a vision of Black tomorrows. They fail when they are expected to supply everything that our communities need for survival, growth, and success on a local, national, and world stage.

Black lives matter, just like Black families, communities, schools, colleges, universities, graduate schools (law, medicine, business, engineering, humanities, science, technology, the arts, self-defense, psychology, etc.) matter. A Black mindset not only states and defines what matters, but digs deep each second, minute, hour, and day of each month and year to do the necessary work that our foreparents—mothers and fathers who proceeded us—left to us to complete. The larger goal is always justice. In recognizing not only our own suffering but that of others. Thereby erasing the fears that keep us apart rather than joining hands to solve problems.

We have become refugees in our own land, not citizens of the country built on the backs of Black people. Today, because we are alive and questioning whether Black lives matter or not, are there also the buts? It is always the buts, the genuine, heartfelt, overworked buts. If we could just get past the buts in our individual and collective lives, maybe, just maybe, we will cease to be a marginalized and dependent people and rise to the occasion and excel in doing the possible and impossible whatever the mission may be. And I am not talking about a *movie*.

Sixteen Shots in Fifteen Seconds

These are the defining questions. What on earth have we done as Black people to deserve the horrific treatment that we have received from white people over the last three centuries? What major transgression have we—Black people, African American, people of African ancestry—committed against white people, European Americans, that has relegated the clear majority of us to a state of total dependency?

For centuries we have suffered deep injustices at the hands of those in power, white power. This white war against Black people in America has never ended. Individual white violence, organized group violence, institutional violence, commercial violence, military violence, and state-sponsored violence all add up to the unceasing acts of national terrorism that have crippled and stopped most serious Black acts of liberation.

The city of Chicago represents one of the major centers of such violence against Black people. Over the last decade the city has paid out over 500 million dollars to settle police misconduct lawsuits. On October 20, 2014, Officer Jason Van Dyke shot teenager Laquan McDonald sixteen times in less than fifteen seconds. A recent video revealed that most of the bullets were shots into his young body as he lay unmoving on the pavement. For over a year, the whole criminal justice system from the mayor's office, police department, to the Cook County state's attorney office attempted to suppress this information.

The video was officially released in November of 2015. Prior to that time, however, the city paid $5 million to Laquan McDonald's family without a lawsuit, Officer Van Dyke was put on desk duty at $80,000 a year, other incriminating tapes were confiscated and erased, the mayor's office, under the guise of letting the federal investigators take the lead, stopped everything locally, hoped that the murder would go away. They—Mayor Rahm Emanuel, police superintendent Garry McCarthy, and Cook County state's attorney Anita Alvarez—realized that if the video was released, Emanuel might not have been reelected, because as we all know, his reelection greatly depended upon the Black community, whom he betrayed time and time again.

We are now in our defining hour. Why do they hate us? Why has being Black in America first and foremost defined our reality before anything else? Charles M. Blow, the columnist and author, writes of the killing of seventeen-year-old Laquan McDonald in the *New York Times* (November 30, 2015). He states: "The only reason that these killings keep happening is because most of American society tacitly approves or willfully tolerates it. There is no other explanation. If America wanted this to end, it would end."

Chicago remains the most segregated city in the United States. The daily violence perpetuated externally and internally is so enormous that it too often falls on deaf ears. By any measurable social indicators, Black people in Chicago and across the nation are at the bottom. A recent report from the University of Illinois at Chicago's Great City Institute confirms that young Black men in Chicago between the ages of twenty and twenty-four represent over 47 percent of the out-of-work and out-of-school population and 44 percent in Illinois. This is compared to 20 percent of Hispanic men and 10 percent of white men in Chicago in the same age group. This was reported by Alexia Elejalde-Ruiz on the front page of the *Chicago Tribune* of January 26, 2016. Take my word for it, our situation is far worse than reported.

This is why *Black Lives Matter* to us. If we do not see and love the value of our own lives, we by our silence have joined our enemies. I will state it one final time—we must have *unconditional love for Black people*. If this becomes an undeniable fact, everything else will fall into place, and the traitors among our own people will finally realize the treachery of their own ways. And those who rally against us will see that we are indeed, one people—Black, self-defined, and ready.

The Six Unconditionals

Clearly, all people and especially formerly enslaved Black people *do what we've been taught to do*, whether such instruction is formal, informal, at the point of a gun, at the end of a whip, in the dungeons of the nation's prisons, its classrooms of miseducation and anti-self, or as sugar in all of its capitalist disguises. This speaks volumes to our current condition.

Our predicament, this national state of affairs that Black people struggle with each day, is man-made. The international philosophy of white nationalism, constructed and practiced as white supremacy and white skin privilege, is the white power train driving this worldview, this culture. To this end, all 86,000 Black churches must again become *liberated zones* for self-definition, self-defense, quality education, economic development, political understanding and enrichment, family and extended family inclusiveness, and spiritual enlightenment that is not anti-self or based upon a fiction that is realized in some distant future and some other *world*. The time is *now* for the six unconditionals:

1. *Unconditional Love*—for self, one's family, one's people, and *all* children. Deep caring for the environment, the planet, and justice. An allegiance to all that is good, right, just, and correct—preserved with integrity and a morality encased in life-giving and life-saving vision, health, wellness, and peace.

2. *Unconditional Courage*—to always question authority, injustice, greed, dishonesty, and corruption. To struggle against the accepted grain of corporate culture. To be creative and innovative and encourage artists and their art, to fight the destructive weather of ill-gotten influence, wealth, power, and unquenchable greed.

3. *Unconditional Search*— for knowledge, hard facts, enlightenment, hidden answers, truth within the truth, moral questions within the deadly noise of corporate consumerism of a buy-and-sell culture. To put scholars and scholarship and academic achievement at the center of our continued quest for liberation. To teach and believe that learning and daily studying are the heartbeats of all enlightened and independent people. We must understand the absolute necessity for strong and outstanding schools, colleges, and universities, that they are essential to our core existence in building a knowledge-based culture and civilization. Art, in all of its creative possibilities, must be at the center of our lifelong learning: poetry, fiction, music, visual art, dance, drama, and all that one can learn in challenging one's mind, soul, and imagination.

4. *Unconditional Will*—to appreciate and be aware of the power of *one* creative individualism. Comprehend the necessity of organizations in the ongoing struggles for political, social, and economic justice. Authenticity, fairness, quality, merit, and excellence should be central to where we want to be. Foundational to all existence is the quality and place of *work*, from the collecting of garbage from urban streets, the harvesting of fruits and vegetables and the production of food on rural family farms to the building of cities, mass transportation systems, healthy living spaces, medical centers, businesses, institutions, sports centers, libraries, art, music, dance, theaters, and relaxation venues. We need all of this and much more for the critical task of creating psychologically and physically whole people. We must never doubt the power or capacity of the human spirit in each person to be creative and to do good. This understanding should be at the apex of our thinking, work, actions, and memory in actively resisting the Americanization and westernization of the world.

5. *Unconditional Wellness*—for health beyond the national norm. Body and mind in concert with the best information, knowledge, and experience available in the world of total body fitness and wellness. Understanding the absolute necessity for personal responsibility in finding, researching, and adopting the best treatment in keeping one's body and mind ready for the many trials, tests, stresses, and confrontations of capitalism and Western culture.

6. *Unconditional Kindness and Empathy*—that which is the underpinning force of a spiritual mindset is kindness itself and empathy toward family and others. Everything and everyone in the world is connected and is in the final and first analysis *one*. The golden rule of all major spiritual forces is "Do unto others as you would have them do unto you." Kindness and empathy are the transcending forces that lead—with spiritual knowledge—to the opening of minds and the most important word in English, *yes.*

March 7, 2018

From Taking Bullets: Terrorism and Black Life in Twenty-First Century America Confronting White Nationalism, Supremacy, Privilege, Plutocracy, and Oligarchy. A Poet's Representation and Challenge

Gellila Asmamaw

Ode to Dawn

Chi-town Native.
cars bustlin, lights flashin
the world keeps spinnin
keeps tickin. tickin
like my brother's   watch.

sitttin at the lake shore
at dawn.
        the beginning of a new
day. still arising from yesterday.
yesterday's fears and sorrows
and crimes and enemies. but
today is a new day
        a new day
a new life. fresh
        start

remember
        the 16 shots

yesterday
        but live a new day
a new dawn. no moon, no sun
just you. it's the start of a new day.
put the shootings away.
        but don't forget
where the hate came from.
remember that hate
and turn it into love
at the start of a new dawn.
it's a new life, so breathe
        and remember

what you're living for.
at the start of a new day.
a new life.
a new dawn.

Kevin Coval

Outro

Hope is a privilege. It requires some distance from terror, some history at times. The time to stop for a moment to look back to see a forward. Hope is a tool in sustaining and resuscitating the long struggle toward equity and justice. Hope is a necessity to unfurl the radical imagination in the public sphere, like a blanket on the grass in Marquette Park, a spot to chill in the city, in the future. We hope in order to see and secure our place in the world and to figure a tomorrow. Hope requires faith. Not blind, but earned. Hope is the faith in the power of your will and vision and body and the collective strength of your family, crew, community, and city.

I see a different Chicago. Hip-hop first hipped me to hop the train to travel the city for sound, to see a battle or piece of graffiti. Because it was Chicago, and hip-hop had not yet rooted here, I heard House and was welcomed by what dance educator & House Philosopher Boogie McClarin calls House's practice of "radical inclusivity." Everyone was at the party. A party created by and for Queer Black and Latinx men that was open for all bodies to come in and get down and get up.

Youth culture is contrarian to the wack practices of adult predecessors. It eschews and sheds them like salamander skin and too many clothes in summer. Going to house, then hip-house, and eventually hip-hop parties in Chicago, I saw the city as it could be, its potentiality and future world. Everyone was there outside the restrictions of their neighborhood or culture. Mostly working-class kids trying to turn up and dance and practice a new art in the new world.

I am privy to see the new cultures young people are making in Chicago. Louder Than a Bomb: The Chicago Youth Poetry Festival is a glimpse, but every Tuesday night aspiring emcees and poets travel one to two hours to hit the open mic at Young Chicago Authors' Wordplay, the longest-running youth open mic on planet Earth. Once there, they lob acute geopolitical critiques at systems of white supremacy, patriarchy, and heteronormativity and sing praises to they mamas & mans & womans and latest linguistic ingenuity as well as dream in the public, civic sphere their vision of a new city that is more robust and just.

I see a Chicago bent on desegregation. A city where young artists take their work directly to the people, circumnavigating multinational corporate record labels to distribute their music for free. A city where young organizers carve and crave community space for bodies and voices disenchanted, disenfranchised, and criminally underrepresented. I am inspired by the empowerment of young activists who create organizations: the Black Youth Project 100, Assata's Daughters, the Let Us Breathe Collective, and many, many more young people putting their bodies on the frontlines of a fight to make Chicago more for all, demanding an end to state-sanctioned violence and terror on Black and Brown communities at the hands of police and white supremacist institutions and prison-industrial complexes.

This is the end of Chiraq and the fight for the future of Chicago, and this text hopefully urges us farther toward that end. "You can't be neutral on a moving train," wrote historian Howard Zinn. And working people in this city are tired of taking an L every day.[1] The Windy City must become the City of Wins. We have no time or room for neoliberalism or white guilt or derisive reactionary homophobic patriarchal and parochial politics. This is movement time. The movement of the future, for the future of the greatest and most problematic city on the planet rock. The whole world is listening and watching how Chicago gets down. And we will not disappoint. Never that.

I see Chicago beginning to understand that its most potent natural resources are the people who dream and hustle here; who roast coffee in Englewood, who continue graffiti education in Pilsen, who farm in Roseland, who set up freedom camps in Homan Square, the army of moms patrolling their neighborhoods rather than police, squads and gang gangs of young artists connecting across viaducts and discipline to create a vibrant, celebratory, resistant youth culture in our young century.

I see a Chicago committed to the work ahead. This city of hope, earned. This Chicago where the many can remain and not be pushed out by the dim and dumb vision of the few. This is our fight to stay and live and love and create a new city where all can work and eat and rise in the morning to see the sun cracking over Lake Michigan like eggs in your mama's kitchen. We work for a new day and fight for a new city. A city for all, a Chicago for the working many, for the masses to remain and prosper and not a playground for the few. One city, not two. Chicago, a radical public, a Republic for which we stand and sit and demand and dream; a city of the future, right now, we are fighting for our lives.

---

* While I am playing on taking the El, the train, "taking an L" means taking a loss.

Second to None: Chicago Stories
celebrates the authenticity of a city
brimming with rich narratives and
untold histories. Spotlighting original,
unique, and rarely explored stories,
Second to None unveils a new and
significant layer to Chicago's big-
shouldered literary landscape.

Harvey Young, Series Editor